PICTURE

Knits

PICTURE Knits

**20 PATTERNS
PLUS HOW TO DESIGN YOUR OWN**

MARILYN RAWLINGS

JANE TAYLOR

Bell & Hyman
LONDON

Published in 1984 by **Bell & Hyman Limited**
Denmark House, 37-39 Queen Elizabeth Street, London SE1 2QB

© Marilyn Rawlings and Jane Taylor 1984

We are grateful to Longman Group Ltd for permission to reproduce the *Bike* design which illustrates the cover of *Family Circles*, Longman Imprint Books.

British Library Cataloguing in Publication Data

Taylor, Jane
   Picture Knits.
   1. Sweaters   2. Knitting — Patterns
   I. Title   II. Rawlings, Marilyn
   646.45'4   TT825

ISBN: 0 7135 2465 0

Photography by Rob Matheson

Designed by Colin Lewis
Diagrams by Hilary Evans
Typeset by Artbase Presentations Limited, London
Colour separation by Positive Colour Ltd, Maldon, Essex
Produced in Great Britain by Purnell & Sons, Limited, Paulton

CONTENTS

INTRODUCTION

*P*icture Knits is for knitters who are looking for new designs to make and for those who want to learn how to create their own. It isn't difficult and you don't have to be an experienced knitter to learn. Picture sweaters are always popular, but are often prohibitively expensive to buy ready made. The obvious answer is to make your own.

Picture Knits is two books in one. The first part gives 20 new picture knits, with instructions and knitting charts for each one. Each of these sweaters was based on an idea suggested by the person for whom it was made. They were all new, individual and personal. In fact two are so personal that names are included in the design. But these can easily be changed, using the alphabet grid on page 107, to whatever name you like.

This collection of picture knits will lead you into the second part of the book, which explains how easy it is to design your own picture sweater. This method of adapting a basic pattern was the one we used as a basis for our sweater designs when we began making picture knits. The grid or chart shows a scaled-down version of exactly how the design will appear on the sweater and forms the knitting pattern too. If you are not confident about tackling your first design it is a good idea to start with a motif or name on a plain sweater. Or to experiment with simple embroidery like that used for the *Sportsmen* sweaters on page 77.

In part two easy-to-follow instructions are given for every stage of designing a picture sweater — from drawing your original sketch to making a chart, calculating yarn quantities, and adding special finishing touches for particular effects. You will be able to make a picture knit at a fraction of designer prices — and to create it exactly as you want it.

COLOUR KNITTING TECHNIQUES

When you are knitting with more than one colour yarn to make a picture sweater, there are several basic techniques to learn so that you can change from one colour to another, keeping the yarns neatly stranded across the back, and crossing them when you change colour in order to avoid a hole.

STARTING A NEW COLOUR

At the start of a row

When changing to a new colour at the start of a row, tie a single knot with the new yarn in the end loop of the row *below* the one you have just finished. Leave a long enough end to thread easily into a sewing needle, so that you can darn it in when the piece is complete.

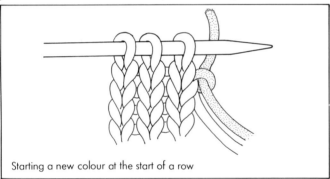

Starting a new colour at the start of a row

In the middle of a row

There are three ways to start a new colour in the middle of a row of knitting:

1 This is the easiest method, but it is not the neatest because it leaves a small knot showing in the row below. Knit or purl to the place where the new colour is to begin, then tie a single knot with the new yarn in the loop below the row being worked. Remember to cross the colours before continuing, to avoid a hole (see diagram). The small knot which appears in the row below can be darned over later during the making up process, to make it invisible. If the two colours are similar this may not be necessary as the knot will not be very obvious.

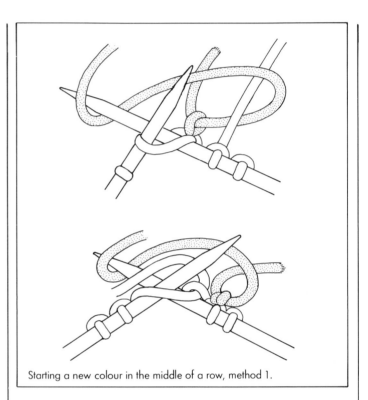

Starting a new colour in the middle of a row, method 1.

2 The second, slightly more complicated, method avoids the knot showing on the work. It is therefore preferable if the two colours are strong contrasts. Knit or purl to the place where the new colour is to begin and put the point of the right-hand needle into the next stitch. Then take yarn A over the top of the right-hand needle, hold it there and begin to knit or purl with yarn B, leaving a long enough end to darn in securely afterwards. The second stitch with yarn B will automatically catch and cross with yarn A at the back to make it secure, and yarn A can then be left behind.

3 The third method is a more secure version of the previous one. Knit or purl to the place where the new colour is to begin and leave yarn A. Put the point of the right-hand needle into the next stitch, then take yarn B with the end under yarn A (to form the important cross which avoids a hole). Knit or purl the next stitch with yarn B with the ball end of the yarn in front of the needle, at the same time making sure that yarn

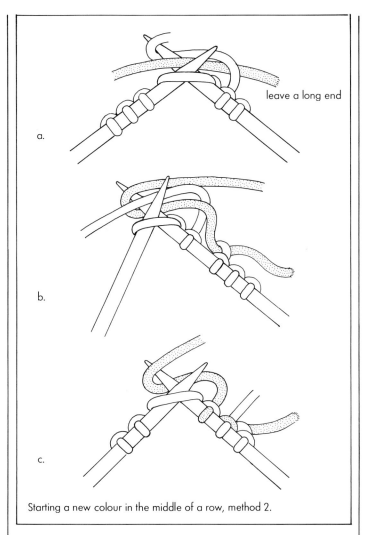

leave a long end

a.

b.

c.

Starting a new colour in the middle of a row, method 2.

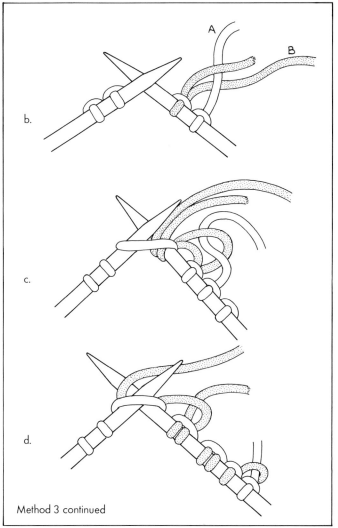

b.

c.

d.

Method 3 continued

A is still between the two strands of yarn B. Knit or purl the next two or three stitches with yarn B double, then leave the short end behind before continuing from the ball end of the yarn as usual. On the return row treat the double stitches as a single stitch each.

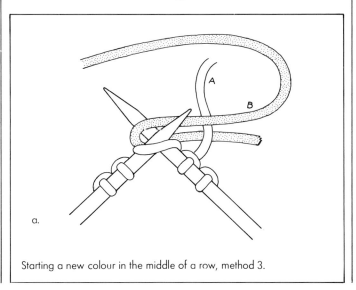

a.

Starting a new colour in the middle of a row, method 3.

STRANDING AND WEAVING

When you are knitting with more than one colour of yarn in each row the yarns have to be carried across the back of the work until they are needed for the next stitch. There are three ways to do this and they all help to keep the back of the work neat and avoid holes where the colours change. The method you choose will depend on how many stitches the yarn has to be carried across. For two or three stitches the stranding method is used. If there are more than two or three stitches at a time in each colour, the yarn must be woven — to stop it hanging in loops at the back of the work. For blocks of colour you should use separate balls of yarn, crossing the colours at the join.

Stranding

When stranding in a knit row, knit three stitches with yarn A, then leave it at the back of the work and pick up yarn

13

B so it strands loosely across the back of the first three stitches. Knit the next few stitches with yarn B, then leave it at the back and pick up yarn A again, stranding it loosely across the back as before. Always make sure that the two colours have crossed at the back before you knit with the new colour, to avoid a hole appearing.

Stranding on a purl row is done in the same way except that the yarns are stranded loosely across the *front* of the stitches you are working.

It is better to strand the yarns loosely because if you pull them too tight the work will have a puckered appearance instead of looking smooth and flat. Practise on a small sample of a picture pattern to get a feel for the correct tension.

Weaving

When weaving in a knit row, knit with yarn A and carry yarn B behind over your left index finger. Place the point of the right-hand needle under yarn B and knit the two yarns together. Yarn B will then be secured behind the work. Do this at three-stitch intervals.

When weaving in a purl row, purl with yarn A and carry yarn B in front over your left index finger. Place the point of the right-hand needle purlwise into the next stitch, bring up yarn B in front of both needles and purl the two yarns together. This should also be done at three-stitch intervals.

Weaving, like stranding, must be worked loosely to avoid puckering and pulling. Practise to get used to this technique if you haven't tried it before.

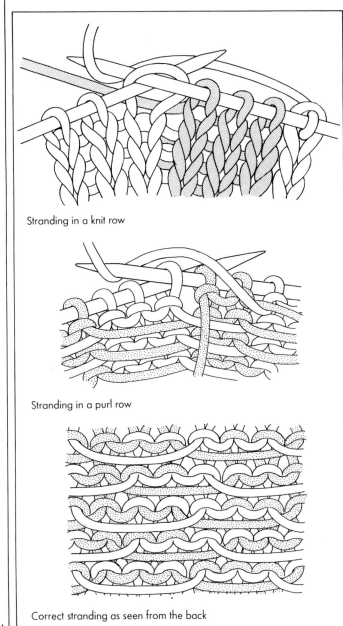

Stranding in a knit row

Stranding in a purl row

Correct stranding as seen from the back

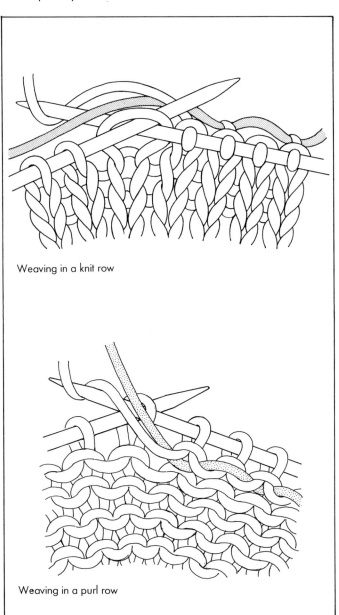

Weaving in a knit row

Weaving in a purl row

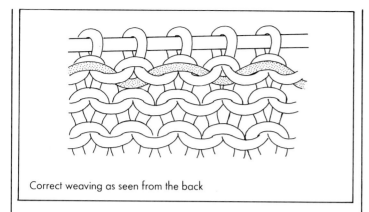
Correct weaving as seen from the back

CROSSING COLOURS

When you are knitting blocks of colour, you should use separate balls of yarn and cross them where they join to avoid holes appearing. The yarns are not stranded across the back. Where blocks of the same colour appear in the same row you will need to wind a new small ball for each block of colour from your main ball of yarn. Do this before you start the row by counting how many balls you will need. Estimate their size by the number of rows to be knitted in each block. Start each new ball in its place across the row, using one of the starting methods already described.

Using a new ball of yarn for each block of colour saves too much weaving or stranding which wastes yarn and can produce a bulky effect if used for large areas.

When knitting colour blocks the yarns must be crossed where they join on every row before starting to knit with the new colour. If you forget to do this a hole will mysteriously appear at the join, which will require darning later to improve the appearance of the finished sweater.

Crossing colours in a knit row

Knit to the place where the two colours join and insert the point of the right-hand needle into the first stitch of the

new colour before crossing yarn A (first colour) over yarn B (second colour) at the back of the work. Then continue knitting with yarn B as usual. Remember to knit the first stitch of yarn B fairly tightly to get a neat join. This is especially important for a vertical join which comes in the same place in each row — if the join is knitted loosely it will pull apart even more when the sweater is stretched in wear and spoil the look of the design. *Cityscape* is an example of a design with many vertical joins.

Crossing colours in a purl row

Purl to the place where the two yarns are to join and insert the point of the right-hand needle into the first stitch of the new colour before crossing yarn A (first colour) under yarn B (second colour) at the front of the work. Then continue purling with yarn A as usual. Again, this first purl stitch must be fairly tight to maintain a neat join in the work.

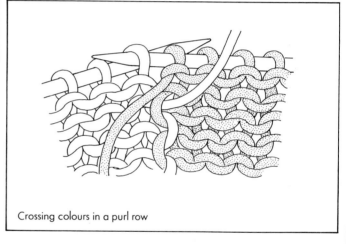
Crossing colours in a purl row

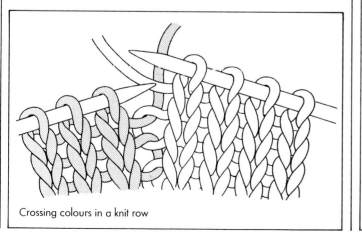
Crossing colours in a knit row

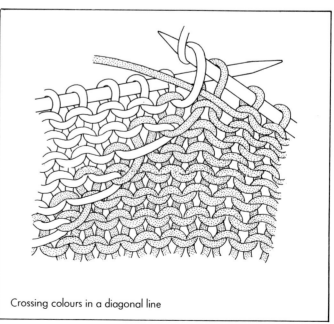
Crossing colours in a diagonal line

DARNING IN THE ENDS

Although you may feel that the inside of your picture sweater is not important it *is* worth spending time neatening and securing all the loose ends of yarn. If any of your joins are not perfect this is a good opportunity to improve them.

When you break off the yarn from a colour you have finished knitting, leave a long enough end to darn in easily when the piece is complete. Short ends are very frustrating to thread into a darning needle. But if you have accidentally left a short end it will be easier to cope with if you slip the needle into the knitting *before* attempting to thread the yarn into it. You should also try to leave a long end when tying in a new colour, because all the ends should be darned in to produce a neat and secure piece of knitting.

1 If you have joined the same colour of yarn in the middle of a row with an ordinary knot, this is best darned in diagonally so that it does not pull out when the sweater is worn.

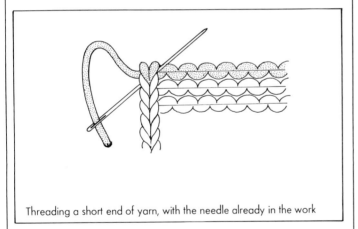

Threading a short end of yarn, with the needle already in the work

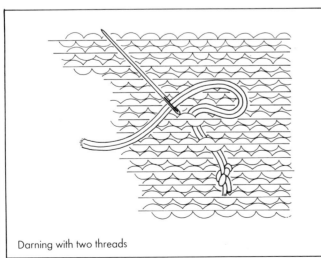

Darning with two threads

2 Ends of yarn where there are blocks of colour can be used to make the joins more secure by overstitching the joins.

3 Ends of yarn at the start or finish of a row can be darned into the edge or oversewn along the edge as they will disappear into the seams of the finished sweater.

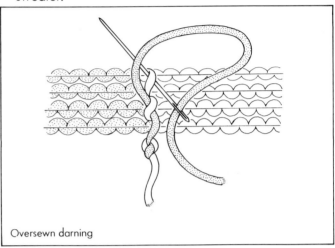

Oversewn darning

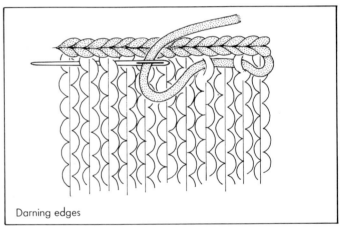

Darning edges

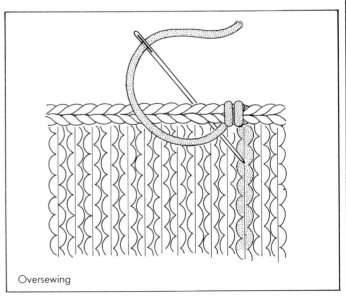

Oversewing

16

Balloon

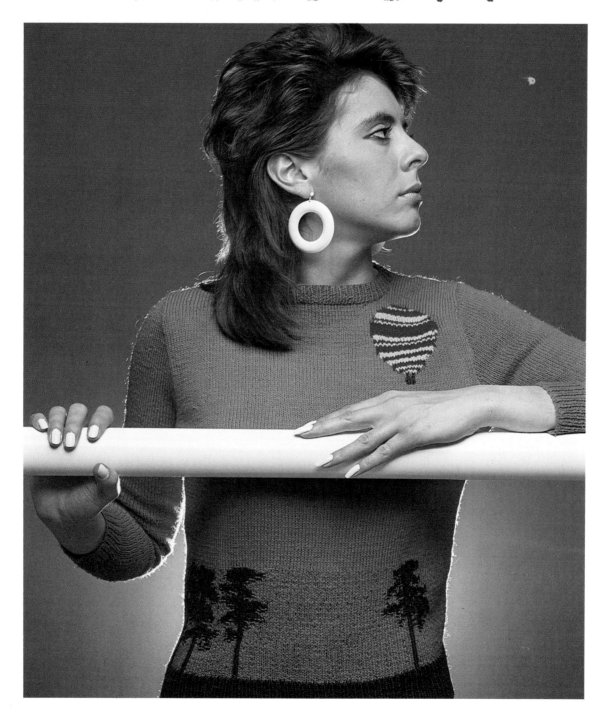

Leopardskin Rug

Bears

STAR WARS

22

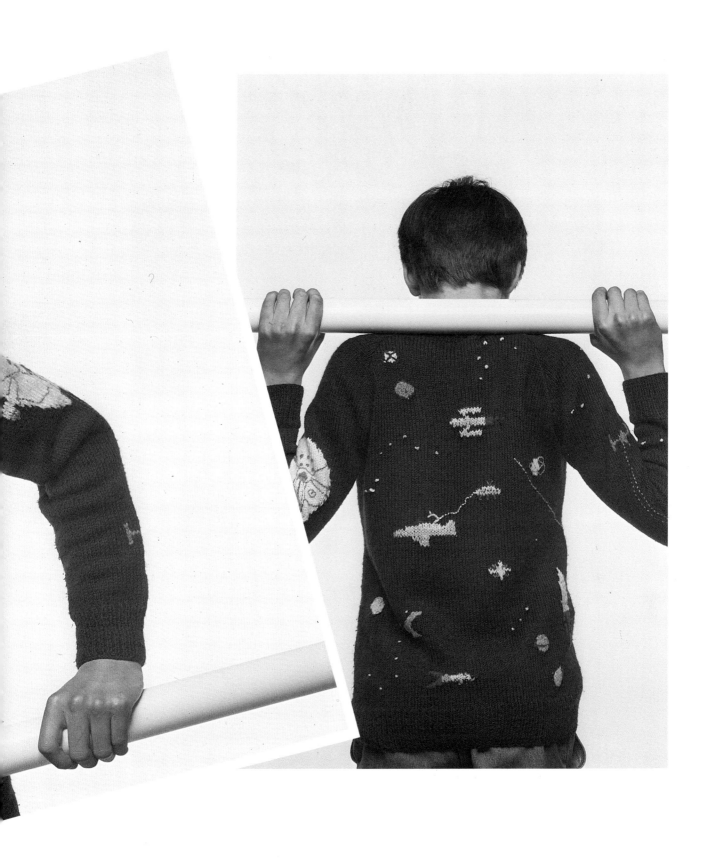

OAK TREE

CAMERA

YORKSHIRE MOORS

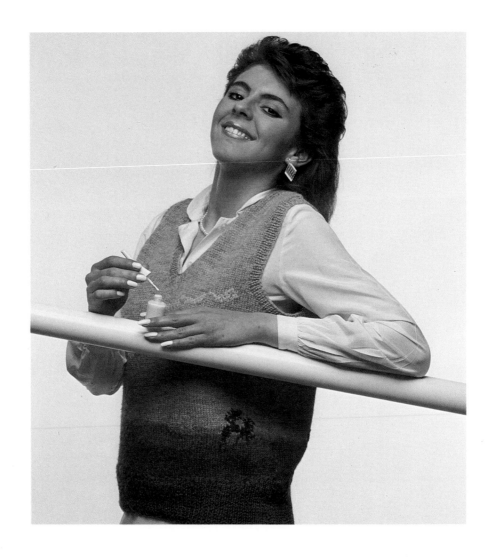

Autumn Stripes

Stormy SEA

Katie's Farm

Woman

SPORTSMEN

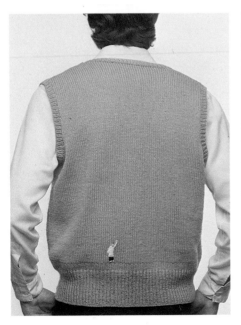

WENDY'S CAT

PALM TREES

BIKE

Sunset Sea

COLOUR BANDS

ANIMAL SKIN

52

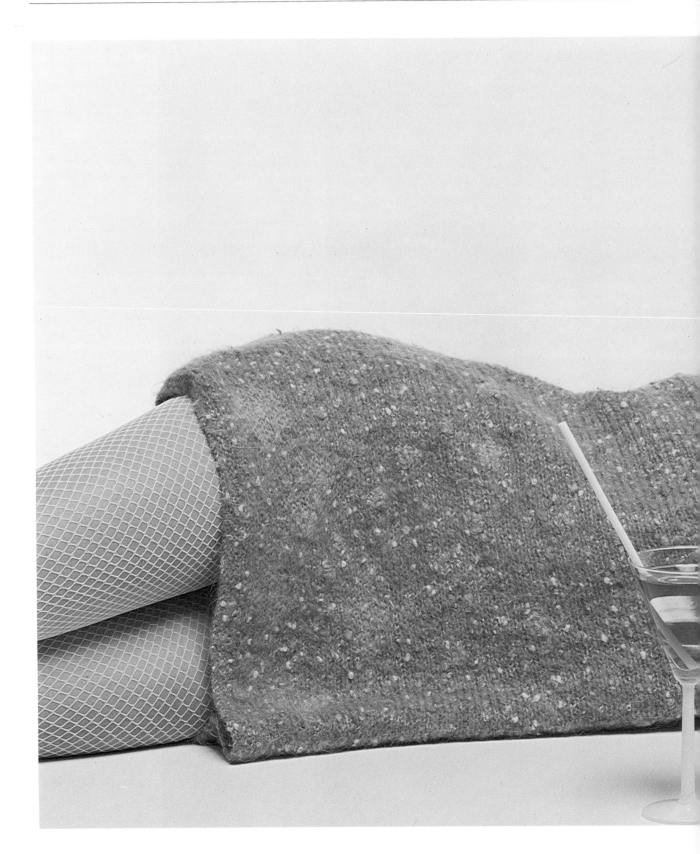

THE PATTERNS

If you haven't knitted from a chart before, you will find it quick and easy to learn how. Each square on the chart represents one stitch, so one row of squares is equal to one row of knitting. Just remember to start following the chart from the bottom right hand corner. This first row, and every odd numbered row, is worked from right to left. The even numbered rows are worked from left to right.

The charts are shown in one size only, but you can check, and if necessary, alter the sizes quite easily. See the section *The Sweater Shape* on page 90 for an explanation.

Two needle sizes are given for each pattern. The smaller needles are for the ribbing and the larger needles for the rest of the sweater.

For instructions on knitting round necks, V necks etc. as you wish, see the basic patterns at the end of the book (page 107).

[See colour page 17]

Turquoise 4-ply sweater, knitted from a single rib mainly in stocking stitch with set in sleeves and round neck. The treetops are in purl.

Sizes to fit 86cm (34in) chest
Body length to underarm 32cm (including 6cm (2½in) single rib)

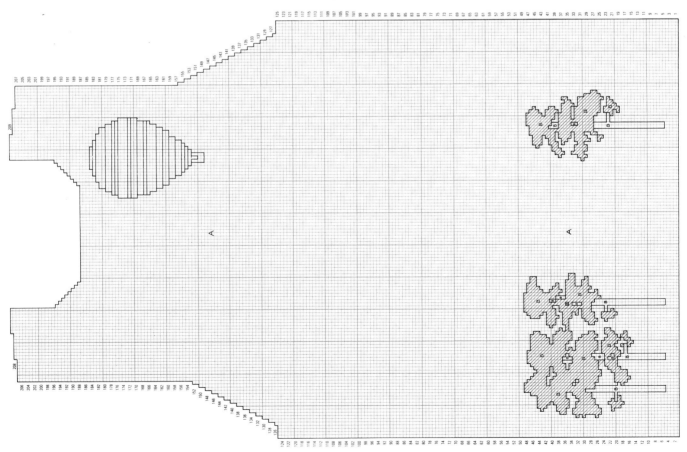

Front 130sts Add rib

Key   Plain ☐
       Purl ☑

Sleeve length 46cm (18in) to underarm

Yarn 4-ply 250g
A: Turquoise 200g
B: Dark Green 50g
Oddments of bright colours for balloon stripes

Needles 3¼ mm (no.10) 3mm (no.11)

Tension 28 sts and 38 rows in st.st. on 3¼ mm (no.10) needles to 5cm (2in) square.

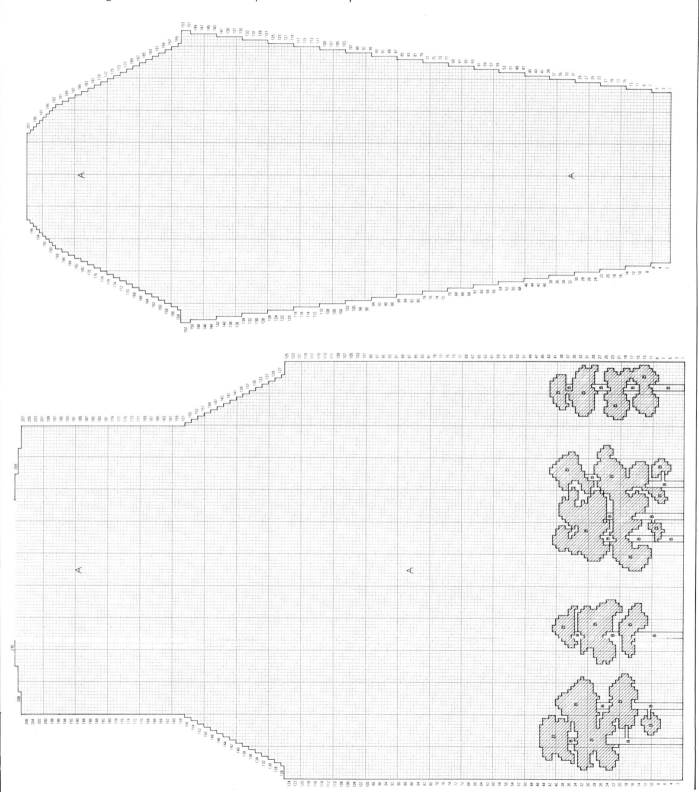

Sleeve (both sleeves are plain) 53sts Add rib

Back 130sts Add rib

Leopardskin Rug

[See colour pages 18-19]

A bold and cheerful design in double knitting in stocking stitch from a single rib, with set-in, puffed sleeves and a collar-effect neckline. The details of the woman's face are embroidered on and there are trims for the special effects, such as the leopard's nose and tongue. Lace trimmings for the underwear, buttons for the suspenders and pom-poms for the shoes are also added.

Sizes To fit 86cm (34in) chest
Body length 40cm (16in) to underarm including 9cm (3½in) single rib

Sleeve length 45cm (18in) to underarm including 9cm (3½in) single rib

Yarn Double knitting 630g

MY Navy Blue	400g	**D** Fawn	100g
A Pink	50g	**E** Black	20g
B Orange	20g	**F** Dark Brown	20g
		(shown as ⊡ on charts)	
C Turquoise	20g	**G** Dark Pink	oddment

Notions animal eyes and nose from craft shop; felt for tongue; strong thread for whiskers; lace or ribbon for underwear trim; pom-poms for shoes (see p.102).

Needles 4mm (no.8) and 3¼mm (no.10)

Tension 12 sts and 16 rows in st.st. on 4mm (no.8) rides over 5cm (2in) square.

Key   Black (E)   ■
          Dark Brown (F)   ⊡

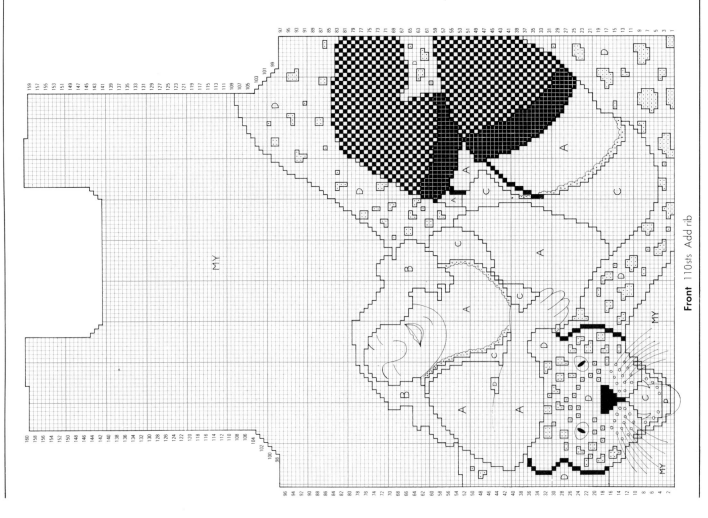

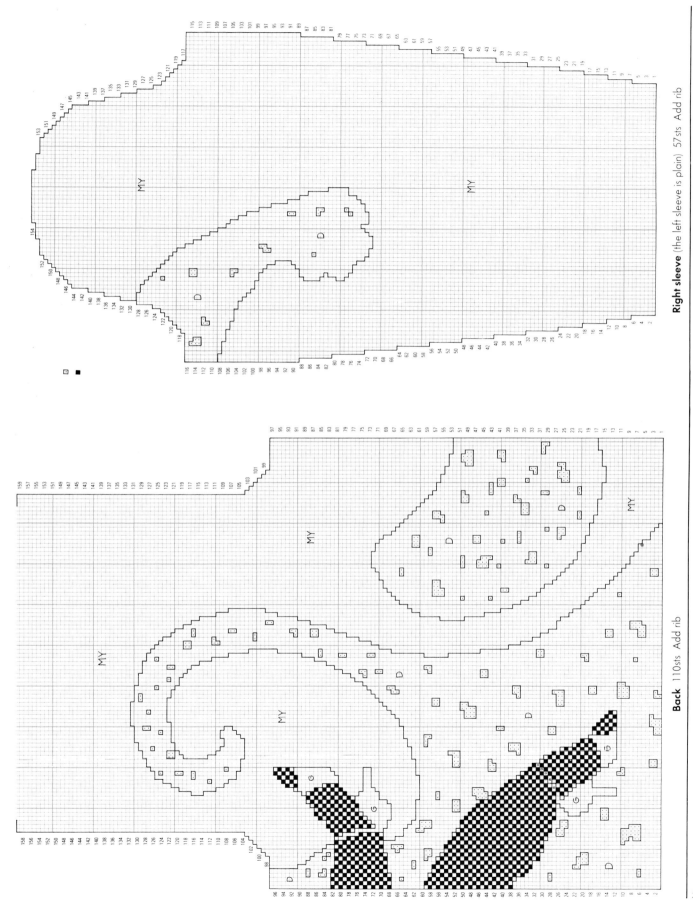

Right sleeve (the left sleeve is plain) 57 sts Add rib

Back 110 sts Add rib

To knit a divided collar

Pick up sts and rib round neckline as usual for about 3.5cm (1½in). Then rib to centre front and turn. Continue on these sts only for desired length of collar, leaving the rest of the sts on the end of one needle or transfer to stitch holder if preferred. Cast off loosely in rib. Rib on sts on other needle for matching depth. Cast off.

The fishnet stockings cre knitted in alternating stitches of black and pink.

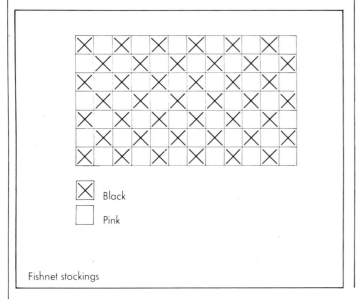

☒ Black

☐ Pink

Fishnet stockings

Bears

[See colour pages 20-21]

A double knit sweater for a bear lover. Knitted from a single rib in stocking stitch with raglan sleeves and a round neck.

Sizes to fit 86cm (34in) chest
Body length 43cm (17in) to underarm including 6cm (2½in) single rib
Sleeve length 47cm (18½in) to underarm including 6cm (2½in) single rib

Yarn Double knitting 550g
MY Brick Red   500g
A Fawn   50g

Needles 4mm (no.8) and 3¼mm (no.10)

Tension 11sts and 15 rows in st.st. on 4mm (no.8) needles over 5cm (2in) square.

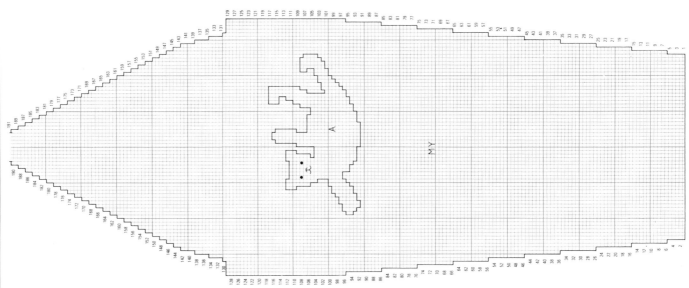

Right sleeve (the left sleeve is plain) 52sts Add rib

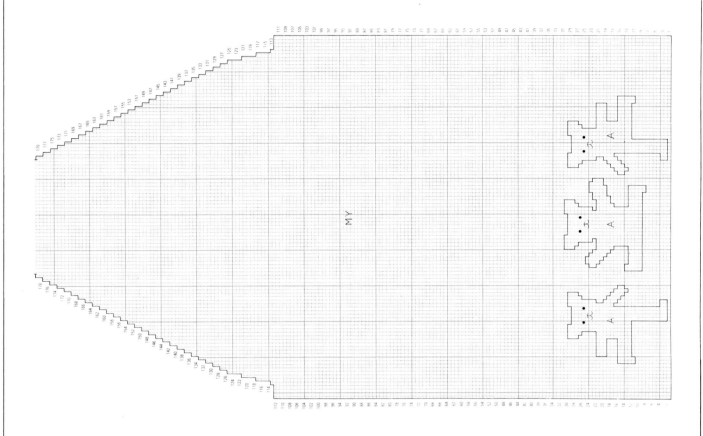

Back 99sts Add rib

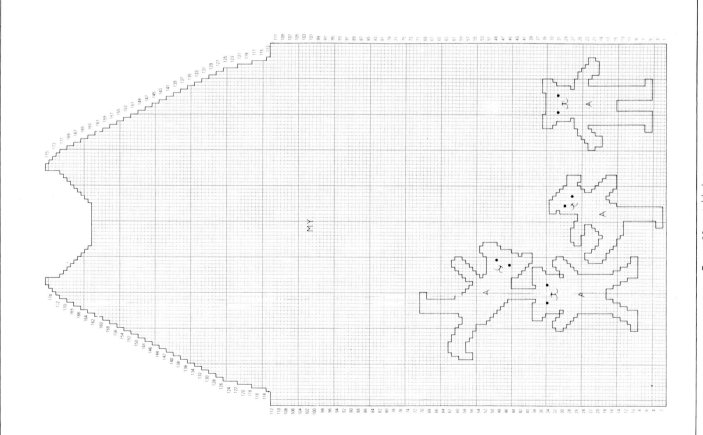

Front 99sts Add rib

61

[See colour pages 22-23]

Space vehicles from the science fiction series doing battle on a night sky background. Double knit sweater in stocking stitch with single rib, raglan sleeves and round neck. The stars are embroidered french knots and the lines of fire and space ship details are sewn in backstitch.

Sizes to fit 86cm (34in) chest
Body length 43cm (17in) to underarm including 6cm (2½in) single rib
Sleeve length 47cm (18½in) including 6cm (2½in) single rib.

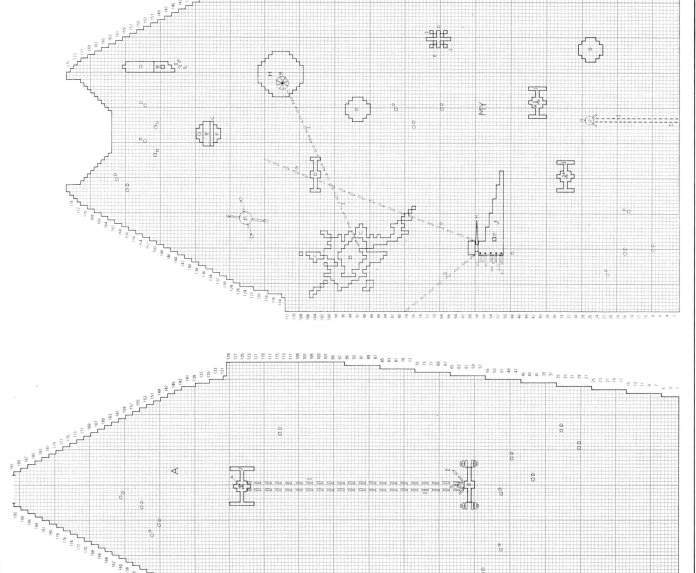

Front 99 sts Add rib

Left sleeve 52 sts Add rib

Yarn Double knitting 550g
MY Navy Blue   **G** Yellow
B Red   **H** Dark Green
C Orange   **I** Light Green
D White   **J** Turquoise
E Pale Pink   **K** Grey
F Dark Pink

Use oddments of bright coloured wools for all the space bodies.

Needles 4mm (no.8) and 3¼ mm (no.10)

Tension 11sts and 15 rows in st.st. on 4mm (no.8) needles to 5cm (2in) square.

Note that the lines of embroidery shown on the charts are *not* knitted.

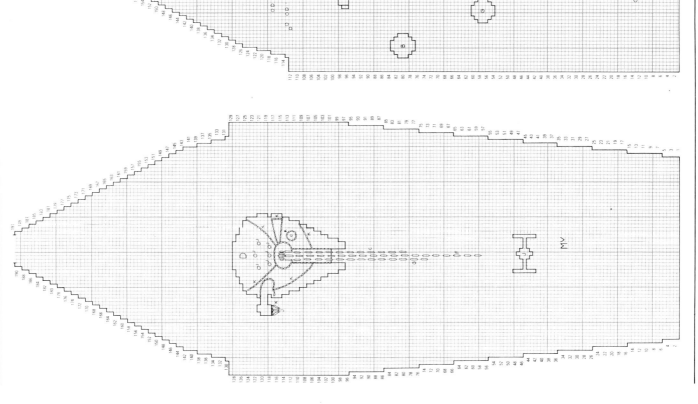

Back 99sts Add rib

Right sleeve 52sts Add rib

OAK TREE

[See colour pages 24-25]

Double knitting slipover in stocking stitch from a single rib with the clouds and leaves in purl. It has a V neck and features a fieldscape on the front and an oak tree on the back, which is embellished with various embroidery stitches.

Sizes To fit 86cm (34in) chest
Body length 32cm (12½in) to underarm including 9cm (3½in) single rib

Yarn Double knitting 240g

Pale Blue	100g	Bright Blue	20g
White (purl for		Blue Grey	20g
clouds)	20g	Lime Green	20g
Dark Green	20g	Navy Blue	20g
Bright Green	20g		

White and Yellow oddments for embroidered sun and daisies

MY Pale Blue
A White
B Dark Green
C Dark Green/Bright Green 'ploughed field' (see below)
D Bright Blue/Bright Green 'ploughed field'
E Bright Blue/Blue Grey 'ploughed field'
F Blue Grey/Lime Green 'ploughed field'
G Blue Grey
H Bright Green
I Bright Blue
J Lime Green

Needles 4mm (no.8) and 3¼ mm (no.10)

Tension 11sts and 15 rows in st.st. on 4mm (no.8) needles to 5cm (2in) square.

The sun and daisies (white with yellow centres) are embroidered on. (See p.99).
The 'ploughed field' effect is achieved by knitting two

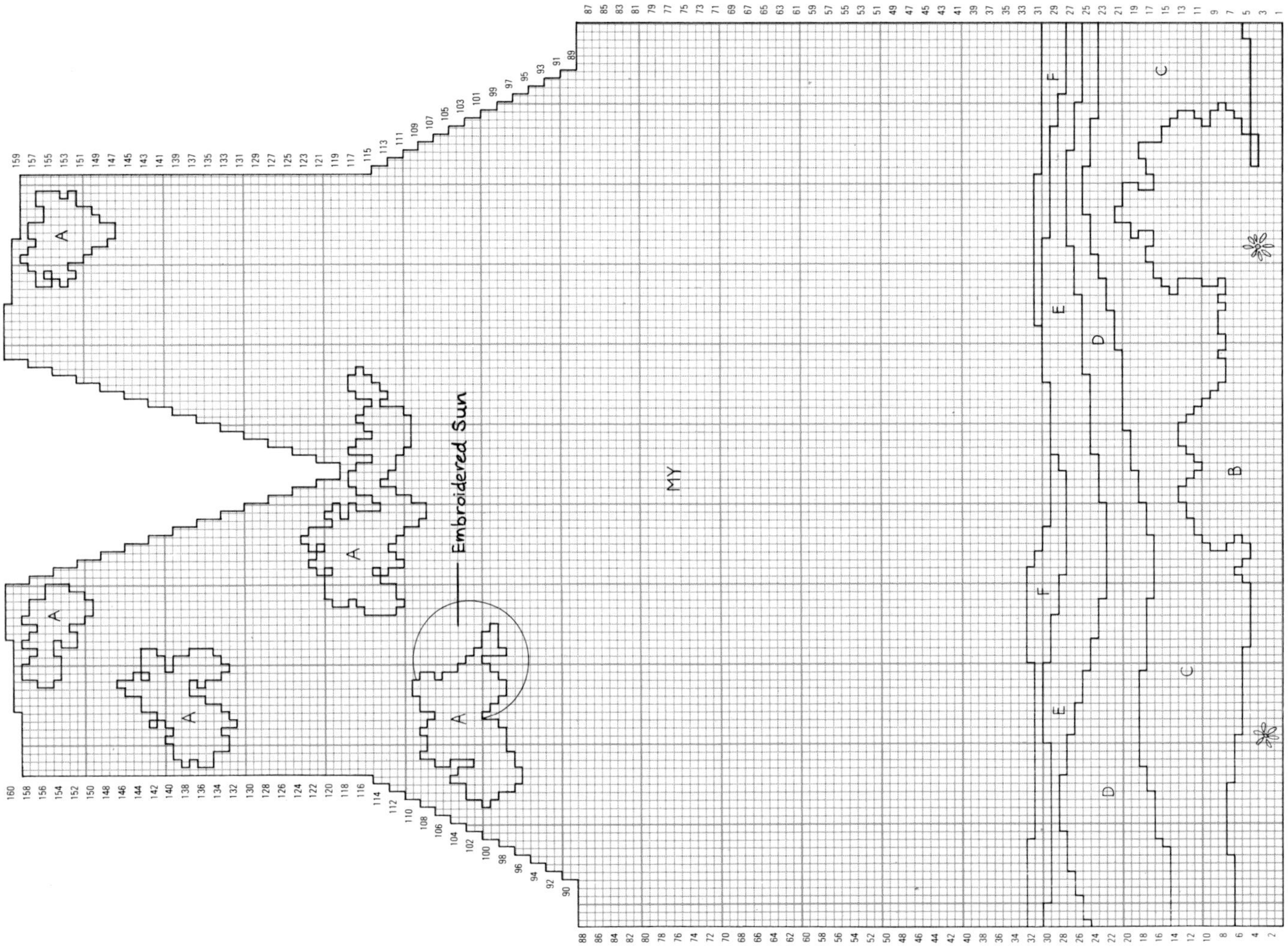

Embroidered Sun

MY

Front 113sts Add rib

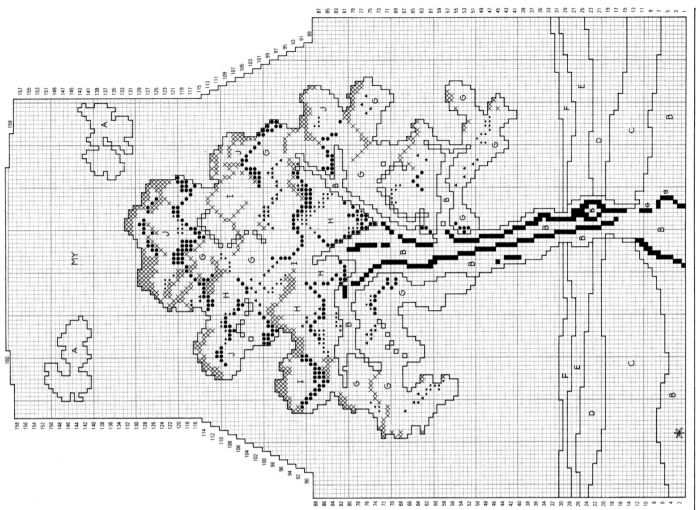

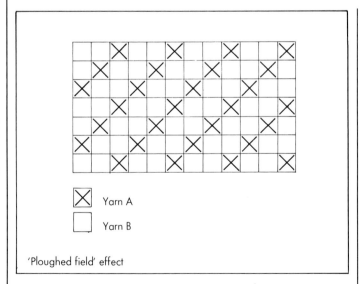

X Yarn A

☐ Yarn B

'Ploughed field' effect

---

chart gives an indication of approximately where the colour changes should come, with little symbols to suggest possible places for contrasting stitches (see the colour photograph). It is the sort of design on which you can use your own imagination and decide what colours you want to put where as you go along.

CAMERA
[See colour pages 26-27]

A sweater for the photographer — the real camera can be worn over the knitted one. Stocking stitch in Double Knitting from a single rib, with raglan shoulders and a round neck. The name of the camera is embroidered.

Sizes to fit 97cm (38in) and 102cm (40in) chest
Body length 43cm (17in) to underarm including 6cm (2½in) single rib
Sleeve length 46cm (18in) to underarm including 8cm (3in) single rib

stitches in one colour, then one stitch in the second colour across the row. On the following row this sequence is repeated one stitch out of step to create diagonal lines (see diagram).

The tree is a blend of the main colours, in small blocks, with a scattering of stitches in other colours across it. The

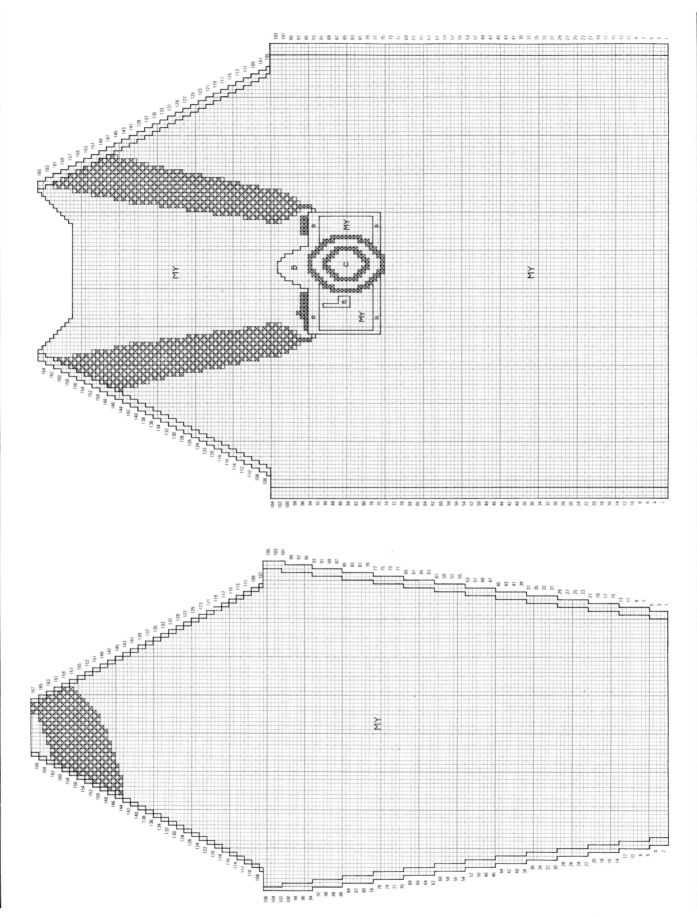

Front 113sts (38in) or 119sts (40in) Add rib

Left sleeve (the right sleeve is the same, reversed)

66

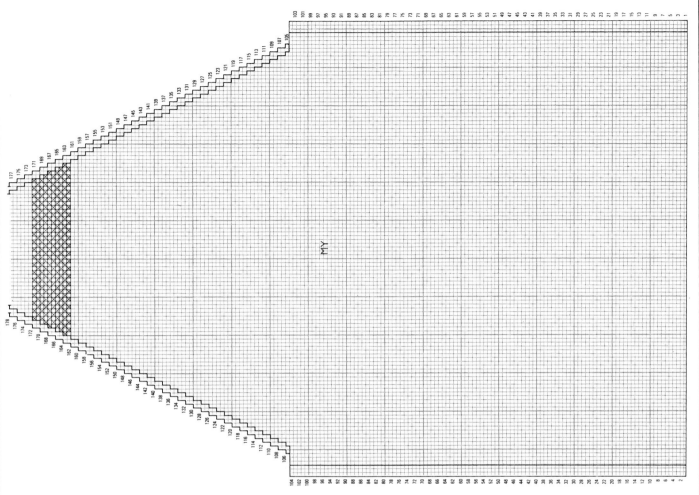

Back 113sts (38in) or 119sts (40in) Add rib

Yarn Double knitting 540g

MY Black	500g	**B** Light Grey		20g
A Dark Grey	20g	**C** White		oddment
marked x on chart		Red for embroidery		

Needles 4mm (no.8) and 3¼ mm (no.10)

Tension 11 sts and 14 rows in st.st. on 4mm (no.8) needles to 5cm (2in) square.

YORKSHIRE MOORS

[See colour paper 28-29]

Slipover in muted Shetland Double Knitting yarn for an appropriately misty effect. Knitted mainly in stocking stitch from a single stepped rib (see page 99) with a V Neck. The stepped ribbing is used to suggest a Yorkshire stone wall. The tree tops are in moss stitch.

Sizes to fit 86cm (34in) chest
Body length 33½cm (13½in) to underarm including 10cm (4in) single stepped ribbing (measured at left side seam)

Yarn Shetland Double Knitting 305g

MY Grey	150g
A Dark Grey	50g
B Mauve	20g
C Blue Heather	20g
D Purple Heather	25g
E Purple	20g
F Pink	20g

Needles 4mm (no.8) and 3¼ mm (no.10)

Tension 12sts and 16 rows in st.st. on 4mm (no.8) needles over 5cm (2in) square

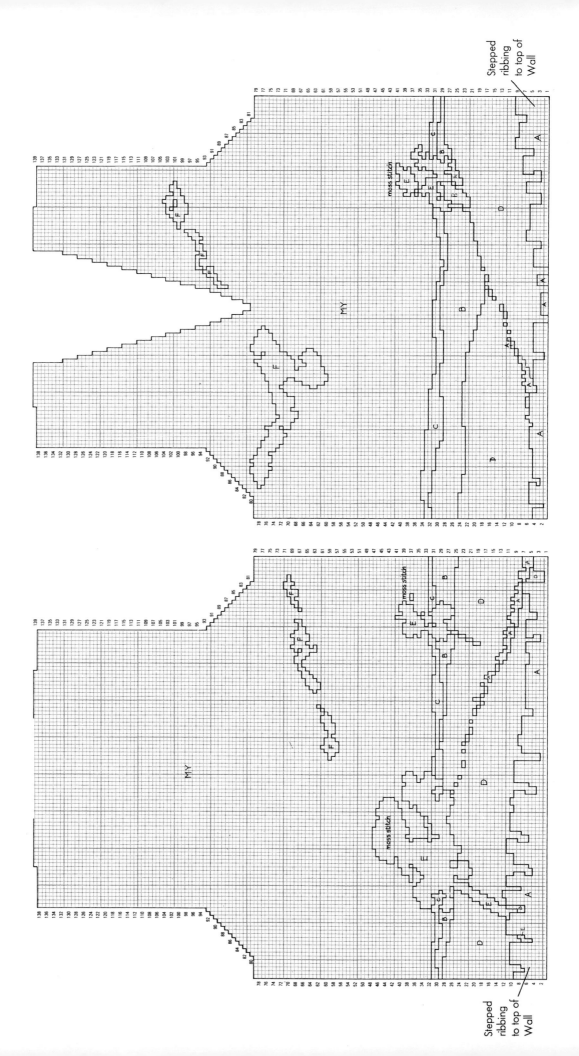

Stepped
ribbing
to top of
Wall

moss stitch

MY

F

F

F

F

E

E

C

B

B

B

C

A

A

A

A

A

D

C

D

A

Front 114 sts Add rib

Stepped
ribbing
to top of
Wall

moss stitch

MY

F

F

F

moss stitch

E

E

C

B

B

C

B

A

A

A

A

A

D

C

D

D

E

E

B

C

Back 114 sts Add rib

68

Autumn Stripes

[See colour pages 30-31]

Jewel colours for a sweater to suit everyone. Knitted in stocking stitch in double double yarn from a single rib, with set in sleeves and a round neck.

Sizes 86cm (34in) chest (loose fitting)
Body length 47cm (18½in) including 9cm (2½in) single rib.

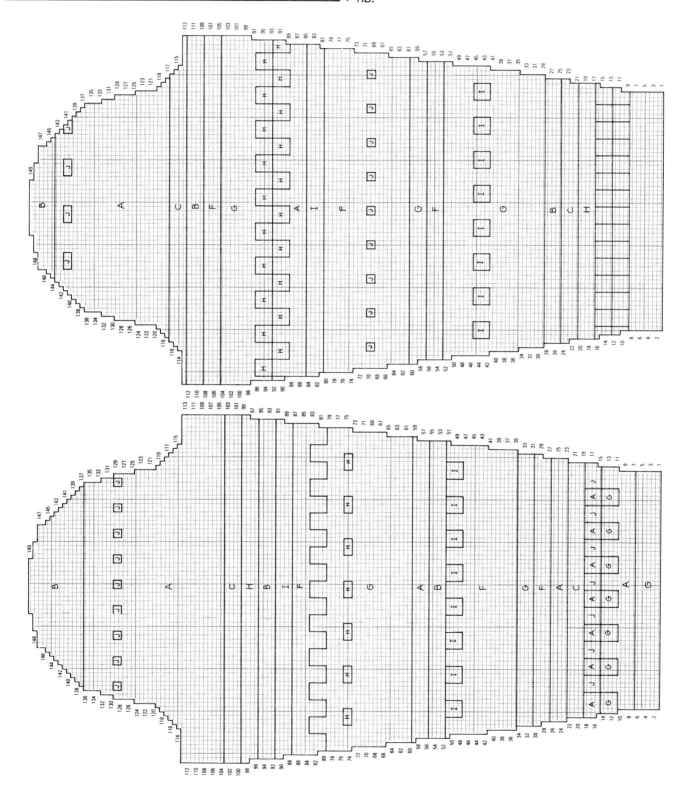

Right sleeve 56 sts Add rib

Left sleeve 56 sts Add rib

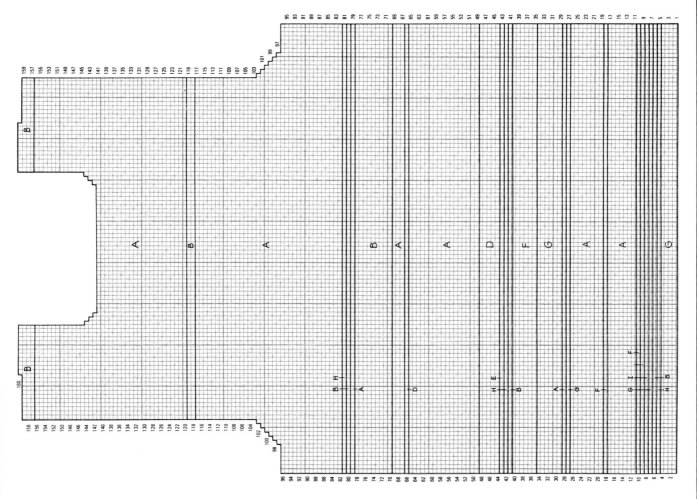

Front and Back (both pieces the same) 110sts. Add rib

Sleeve length 53cm (21in) including 9cm (2½in) single rib.

Yarn Double Double 745g
A Magenta — 300g
B Brick — 50g
C Blue (Prussian) — oddment
D Blue (Cobalt) — 50g
E Green — oddment
F Rust — 50g
G Pink — 200g
H Violet — 25g
I Orange — 50g
J Red — 20g

Needles 4mm (no.8) and 3¼mm (no.10)

Tension 10 sts and 12 rows in st.st. on 4mm (no.8) needles to 5cm (2in) square.

[See colour pages 32-33]

Storm coloured double knit sweater in stocking stitch from a single-rib with set in sleeves and round neck. The foam flecks and driving rain are embroidered on afterwards.

Sizes to fit 86cm (34in) chest
Body length 39cm (15½in) including 7½cm (3in) single rib
Sleeve length 46cm (18in) to underarm including 7½cm (3in) single rib.

Yarn Double knitting 650g
A White — Oddment 20g
B Darkest Green — 70g
C Darkest Blue — 70g

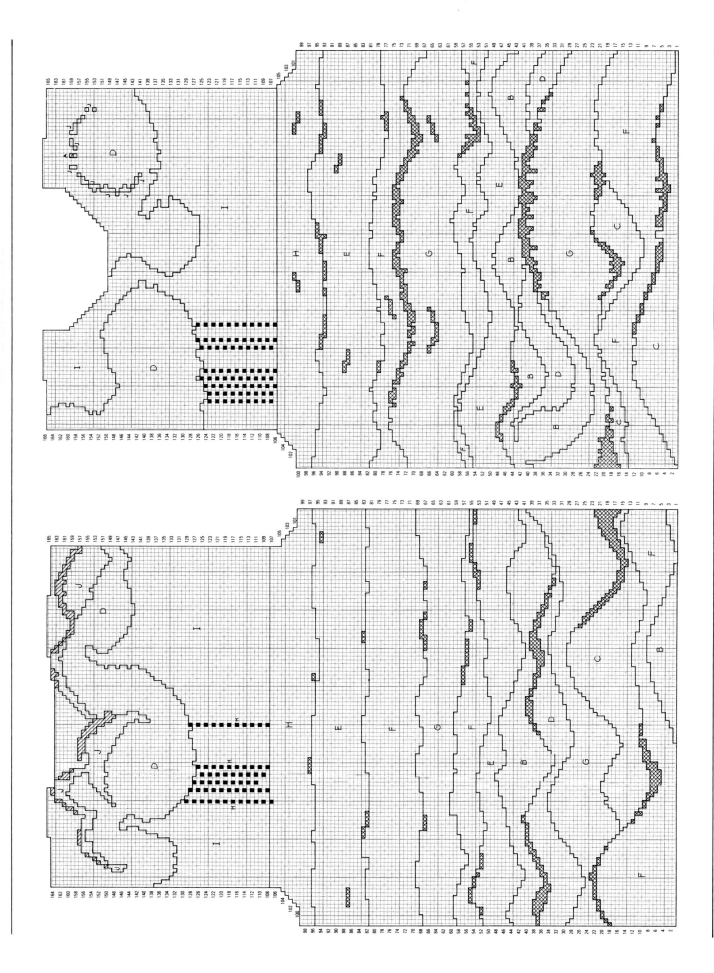

Front 109sts Add rib

Back 109sts Add rib

71

Key
- ☐ Knit in white
- ☒ Purl in white
- ■ Raindrops embroidered in grey

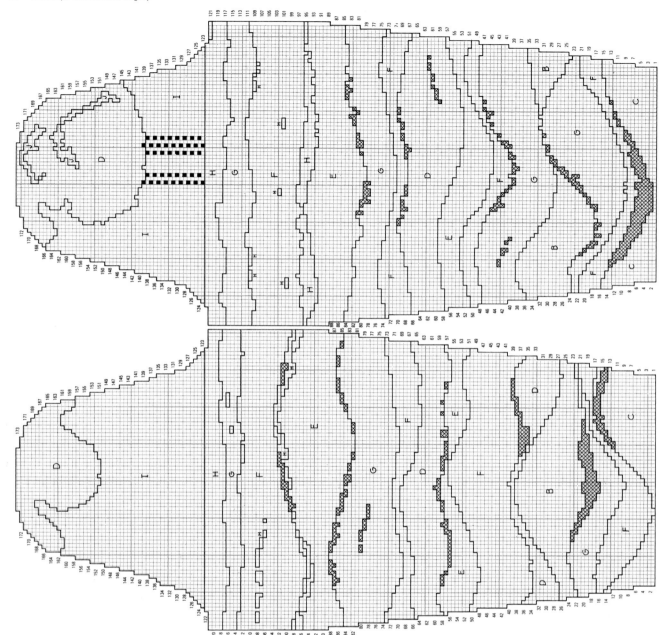

Left sleeve 58sts Add rib

Right sleeve 58sts Add rib

D Purple	70g	
E Bright Green	70g	
F Bright Blue	70g	
G Grey/Blue	70g	
H Pale Green	70g	
I Slate Grey	70g	
J Pale Grey	70g	

Bottom and sleeve ribs in **C**
Neck rib in **I**

Needles 4mm (no.8) and 3¼mm (no.10)

Tension 12sts and 16 rows in st.st. on 4mm (no.8) needles to 5cm (2in) square.

72

Katie's Farm

[See colour pages 34-35]

Sweater designed for Katie who lives on a farm, featuring her own dog on the back. Knit any other name on the gate using the alphabet chart on p.107, adjusting the length of the fence if necessary, or omit the name and continue the line of the fence. Sweater in Double Knit yarn knitted from a single rib mainly in stocking stitch, with set-in sleeves and a collar-effect neckline. Embroidery is

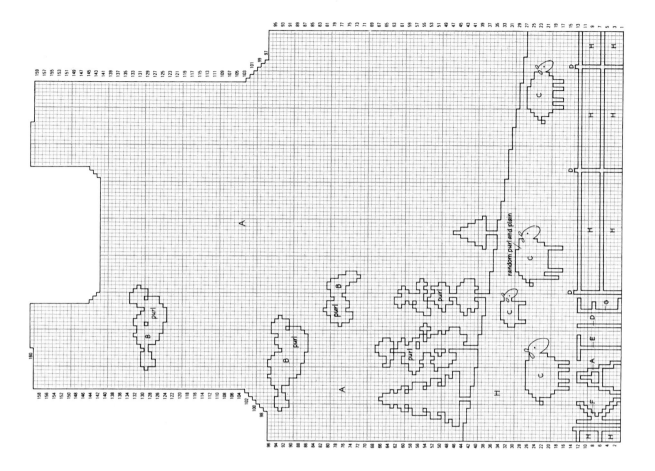

Front 111 sts Add rib

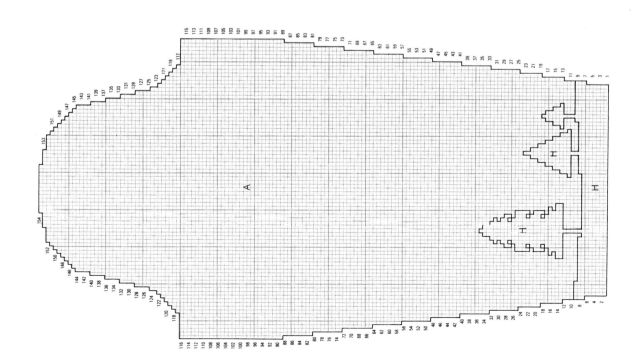

Right sleeve 57 sts Add rib

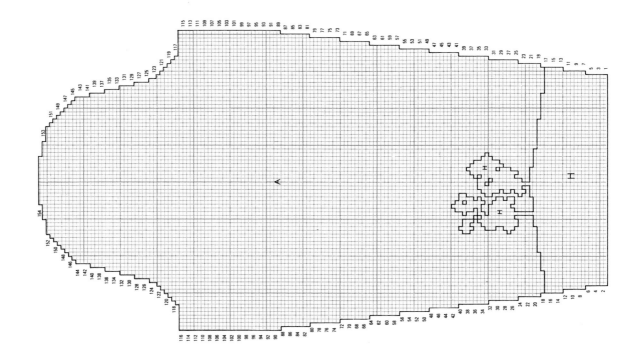

Back 111 sts. Add rib

Left sleeve 57 sts. Add rib

added for details on the dog and sheep. The fence is knitted in dishcloth cotton for a firmer texture, and the clouds in fluffy baby yarn. The trees and clouds are in purl.

Sizes to fit 86cm (34in) chest
Body length 40cm (16in) to underarm including 9cm (3½in) single rib
Sleeve length 45cm (18in) to underarm including 9cm (3½in) single rib

Yarn Double Knitting 680g

MY Pale Blue	450g		**E** Pink	oddment
A Brown	20g		**F** Red	oddment
B Fluffy White	20g		**G** Yellow	oddment
C Arran (off white)	20g		**H** Green	150g
D Dishcloth white	20g		**I** Black	oddment

And oddments of other colours for embroidery

Needles 4mm (no.8) and 3¼mm (no.10)

Tension 12 sts and 16 rows in st.st. on 4mm (no.8) needles over 5cm (2in) square.

For instructions on knitting a divided collar see *Leopardskin Rug* on page 60.

[See colour pages 36-37]

Bright green background for an inviting blonde lady. Sweater in double knitting is worked in stocking stitch from a single rib and has set-in sleeves and a round neck. It could be lengthened to form a dress with the addition of fishnet stockings to the design. The underwear is trimmed with lace/ribbon and the features are embroidered. The lips are done in satin stitch for a full and pouting effect (see p.100).

Sizes to fit 86cm (34in) chest
Body length 41cm (16½in) to underarm including 9cm (3½in) single rib
Sleeve length 45cm (18in) to underarm including 9cm (3½in) single rib
Longer version: Body length 56cm (22in) including 9cm (3½in) single rib

Yarn Double knitting 585g (longer version 645g)

MY Bright green	450g (470g)		**A** Pink	50g (70g)
			B Black	20g (40g)

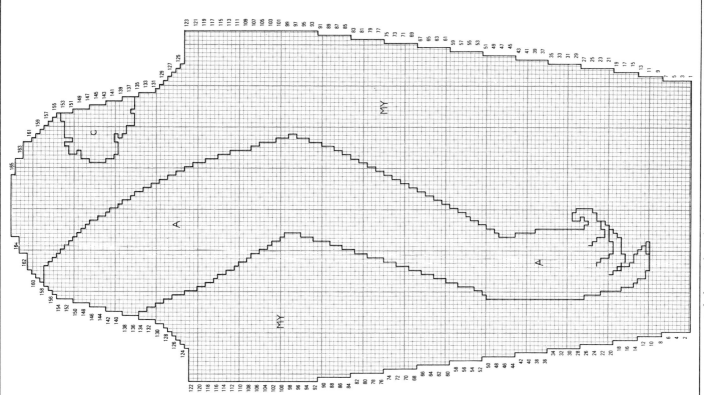

Left sleeve (the right sleeve is plain) 61sts Add rib

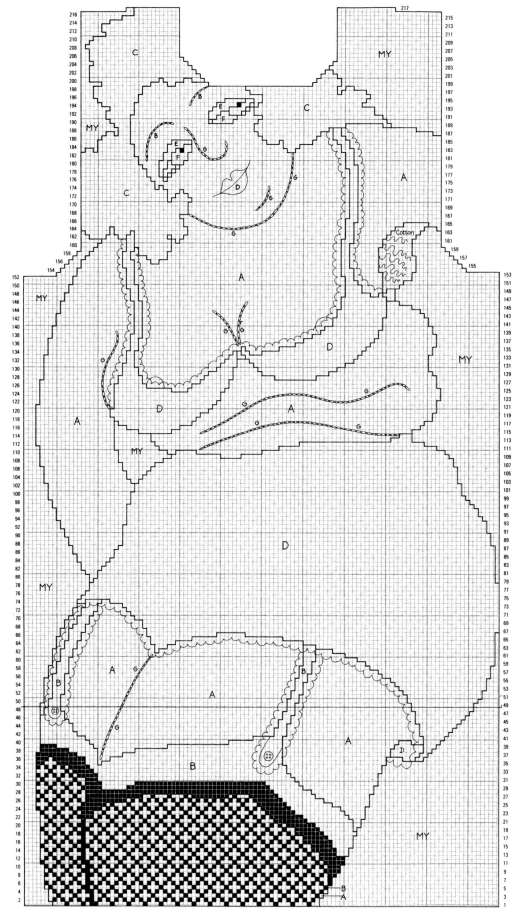

Front (the back is plain) 115sts Add rib

C Yellow   25g (25g)
D Red   40g (40g)
E Light Blue   oddment
F Dark Blue   oddment
G Dark Pink   oddment

Notions Ribbon or lace for underwear trim

Needles 4mm (no.8) and 3¼ mm (no.10)

Tension 12 sts and 16 rows in st.st. on 4mm (no.8) needles to 5cm (2in) square.

The fishnet stockings are knitted with alternating black and pink stitches in a checkerboard pattern. See *Leopardskin Rug* p.58.

SPORTSMEN
[See colour pages 38-39]

Sporting figures embroidered on Double Knit slipovers in stocking stitch knitted from a single rib, with V necks.

Sizes to fit 97cm (38in) chest
Body length 31cm (12½in) including 6cm (2½in) single rib

Bowler (for front of cricket sweater) Position his bottom knee 8 sts up from the green line, and his outermost foot 8 sts in from the right seam.

Yarn Double Knitting 250g
Football — **MY** Dark Blue
Cricket — **MY** Light Blue
Small ball of contrast for pitch line and different coloured scraps for embroidery.

Needles 4mm (no.8) and 3¼ mm (no.10)

Tension 11 sts and 15 rows in st.st. on 4mm (no.8) needles to 5cm (2in) square.

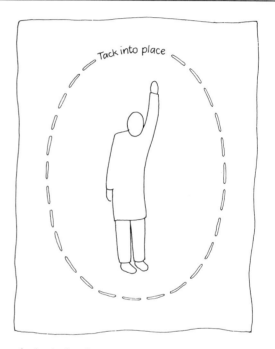

Umpire (for back of cricket sweater) Position his feet on the green line, 40 sts in from the left seam.

Shooter (for front of football sweater) Position his lower foot one stitch above the green line and 21 sts in from the left seam.

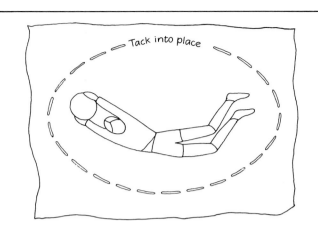

Tack into place

Goalkeeper (for back of football sweater) Position the ball 27 sts in from left seam, and position lower edge of the figure 10 sts above the green line.

Sketch the motifs on paper first. Then tack the paper patterns in position on the sweater, embroider over them in your chosen colours and finally remove the paper. See page 101.

Cityscape

[See colour pages 40-41]

City buildings and a busy river scene. Double Knit sweater in stocking stitch knitted from a single rib with set in sleeves and round neck. Small details of embroidery for clock face, windows and personalised boat and aeroplane.

Sizes to fit 91cm (34in) chest
Body length 35½cm (14in) including 9cm (3½in) single rib
Sleeve length 43cm (17in) including 9cm (3½in) single rib

Yarn Double Knitting 580g

A Crimson	20g	**C** Grey/Green	20g
B Brick	20g	**D** Dark Grey	20g

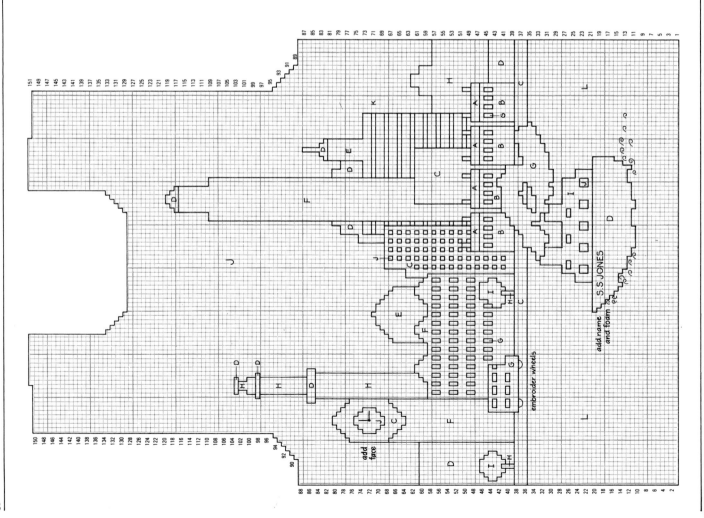

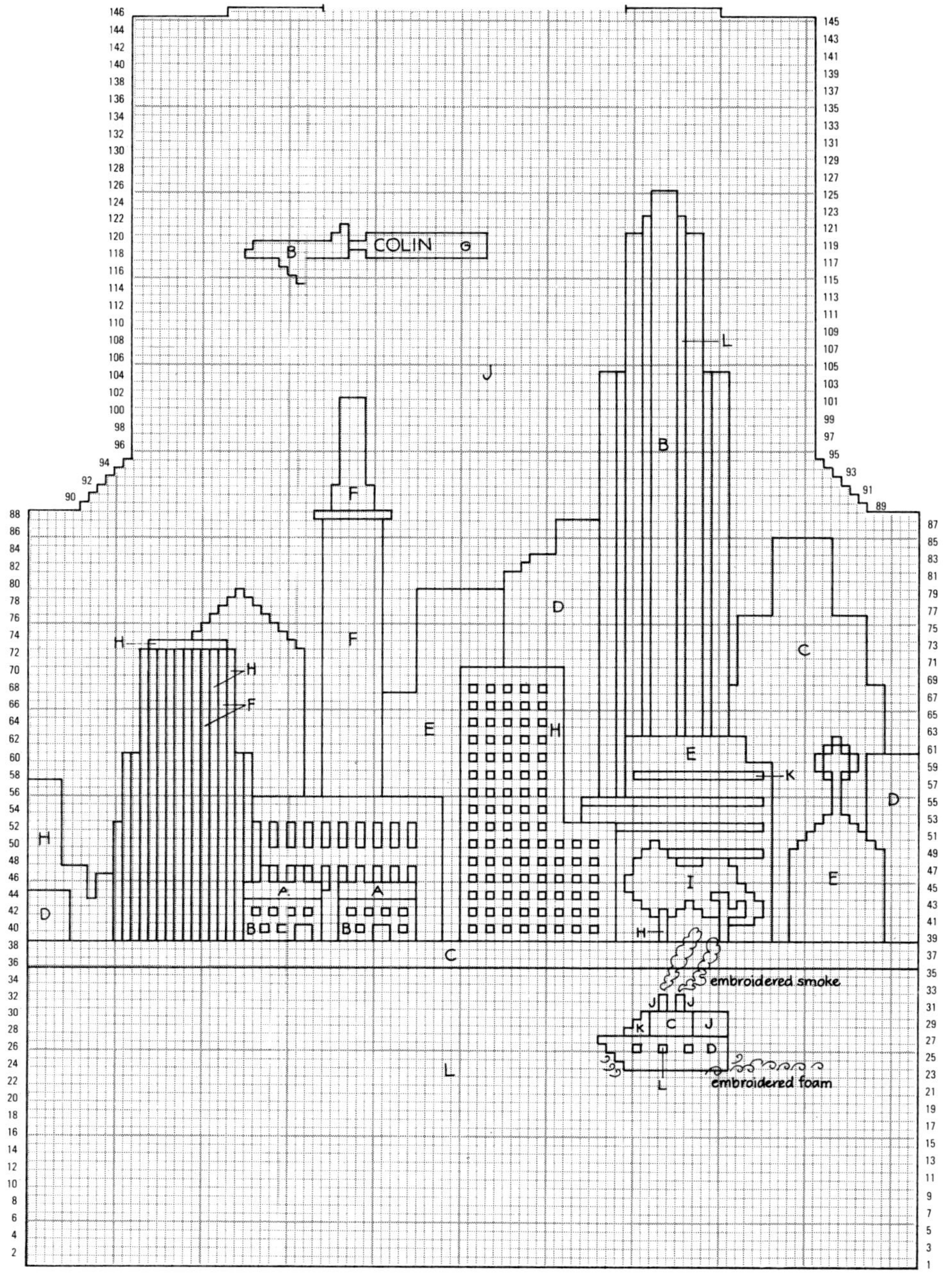

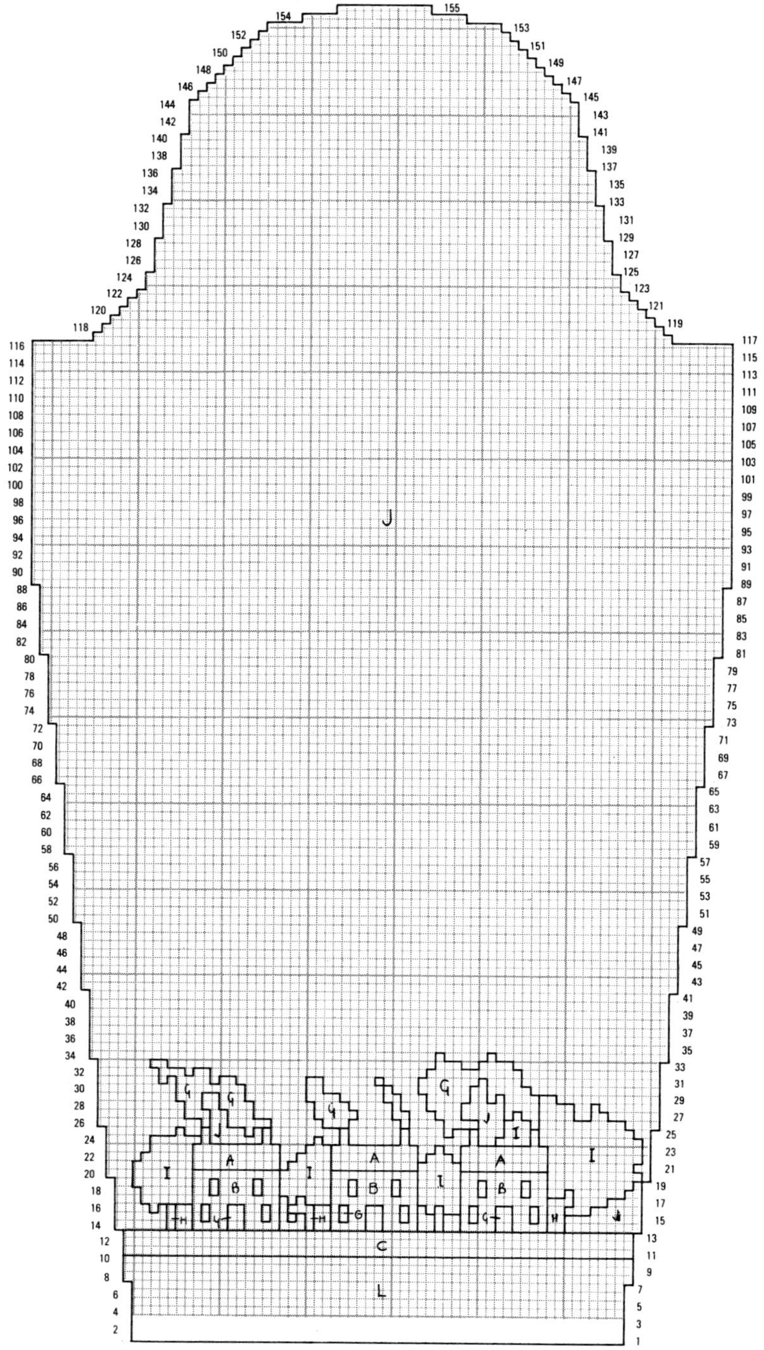

Left sleeve (the right sleeve is the same, reversed) 55sts Add rib

Back 103sts Add rib

embroidered smoke

embroidered foam

COLIN

79

E Beige	20g	**I** Bright Green	20g
F Mauve	20g	**J** Sky Blue	300g
G White	oddment	**K** Light Grey	20g
H Dark Blue/Grey	20g	**L** River Blue	100g

Needles 3¼ mm (no.10) and 4mm (no.8)

Tension 12 sts and 16 rows in st.st. on 4mm (no.8) needles to 5cm (2in) square.

The pattern around the cuff of the left sleeve (see chart) is the same in reverse for the right sleeve.

WENDY'S CAT

[See colour pages 42-43]

Wendy asked for her two favourite things for her sweater — sweets and her cat. You can knit any other name using the alphabet chart on p.107. The sweater is knitted in stocking stitch using double knitting yarn from a single rib. It has dropped shoulders and a round neck. Single rows of colour cheer up a plain rib at the neck.

Sizes to fit 70cm (26in) chest
Body length 28cm (11in) to underarm including 3½cm (1½in) in single rib
Sleeve length 30cm (12in) to underarm including 5cm (2in) in single rib

Yarn Double Knitting 210g
MY Navy Blue	130g
A Pink	20g
B Yellow	20g
C Pale Green	20g
D Pale Blue	20g
E White	40g

Needles 4mm (no.8) and 3¼ mm (no.10)

Tension 12 sts and 16 rows in st.st. on 4mm (no.8) needles over 5cm (2in) square.

80

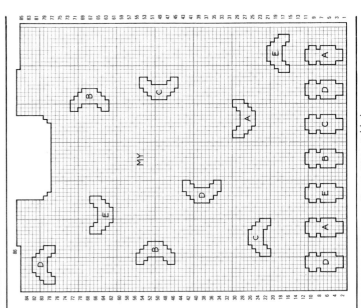

Front 70sts Add rib

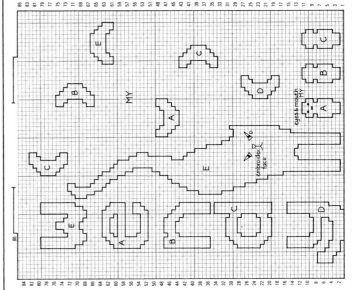

Back 70sts Add rib

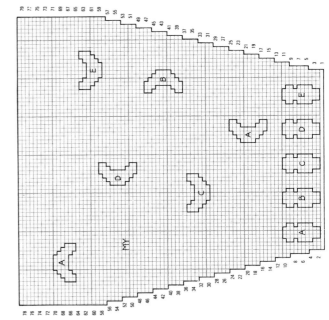

Sleeve (both done the same)

PALM TREES

[See colour pages 44-45]

A tropical jungle and one of the inhabitants, in brilliant shades of green. Leave out the monkey for a more sophisticated effect. Sweater in double knitting is knitted from a single rib in stocking stitch with set-in sleeves and a round neck. Some embroidery is added for the rings on the tree trunks and details of the monkey. Knit monkey in D then embroider with E in satin stitch.

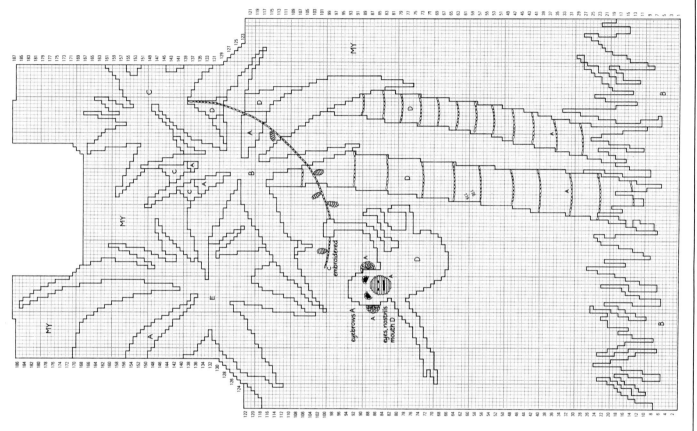

Front 109 sts   Add rib

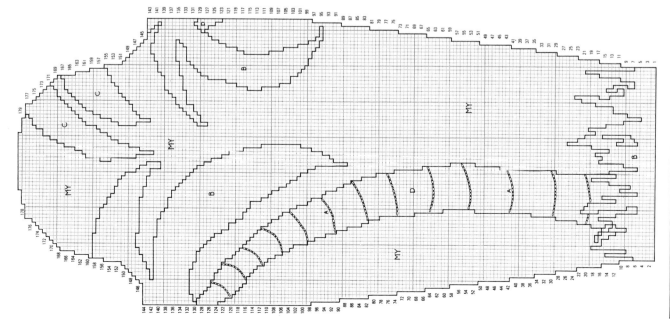

Right sleeve (the left sleeve is plain except for the grass)
54 sts   Add rib

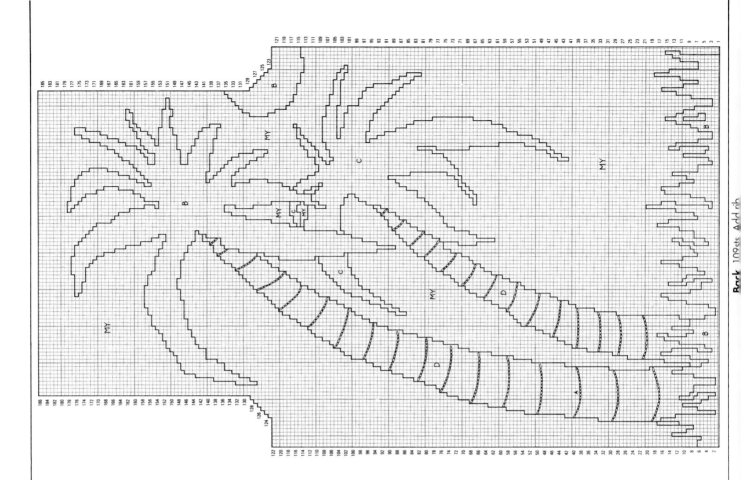

Back 109 sts Add rib

Sizes to fit 86cm (34in) chest

Sizes to fit 86cm (34in) chest
Body length 47cm (18½in) to underarm including 9cm (3½in) single rib
Sleeve length 52cm (21in) to underarm including 7½cm (3in) single rib

Yarn Double Knitting 600g
MY Pale Green   200g
A Fawn   100g
B Mid Green   100g
C Dark Green   100g
D Mid Brown   100g
E Dark Brown (mohair, oddment for embroidery)

Needles 4mm (no.8) and 3¼mm (no.10)

Tension 12 sts and 16 rows in st.st. on 4mm (no.8) needles over 5cm (2in) square.

82

[See colour pages 46-47]

A bright slipover to have fun in. Knitted in stocking stitch using double knitting yarn it features a single rib and a V neck. Embroidery is used to fill in the half stitches of the bike's diagonals, making it appear more realistic.

Sizes to fit 76cm (30in) chest
Body length 20cm (11in) to underarm including 5cm (2in) single rib

Yarn Double Knitting 300g
MY Blue   150g   **B** White   50g
A Green   80g   **C** Red   20g

Needles 4mm (no.8) and 3¼mm (no.10)

Tension 11 sts and 15 rows in st.st. on 4mm (no.8) needles over 5cm (2in) square

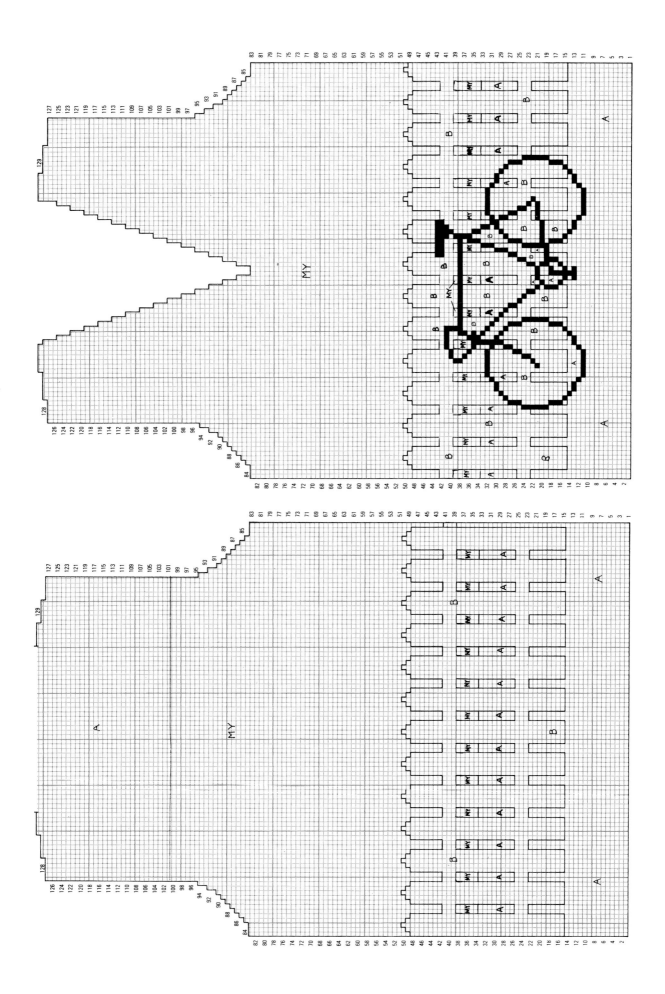

Front 90sts Add rib

Back 90sts Add rib

Sunset Sea

[See colour pages 48-49]

Setting sun colours over the sea for a Double Knit sweater in stocking stitch with dropped shoulders and a divided collar, knitted from a double rib.

Sizes to fit 86cm (34in) chest
Body length 60cm (24in) to shoulder including 9cm (3½in) double rib

Sleeve length 42cm (17in) including 6cm (2½in) double rib.

Yarn Double Knitting 750g
A Dark Blue   200g
B White   100g
C Medium Blue   100g
D Pink   100g
E Grey/Blue   100g
F Pale Grey   200g

Needles 3¾mm (no.9) and 3¼mm (no.10)

Tension 13 sts and 14 rows in st.st. on 3¾mm (no.9) needles to 5cm (2in) square.

For instructions on knitting the divided collar, see *Leopardskin Rug,* page 60.

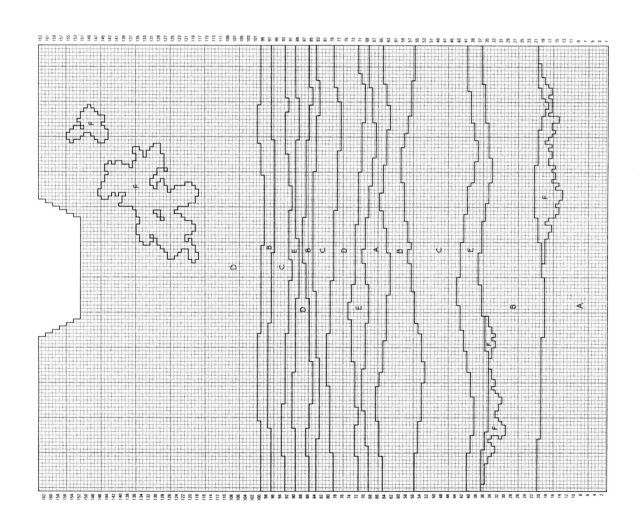

Front 127 sts Add rib

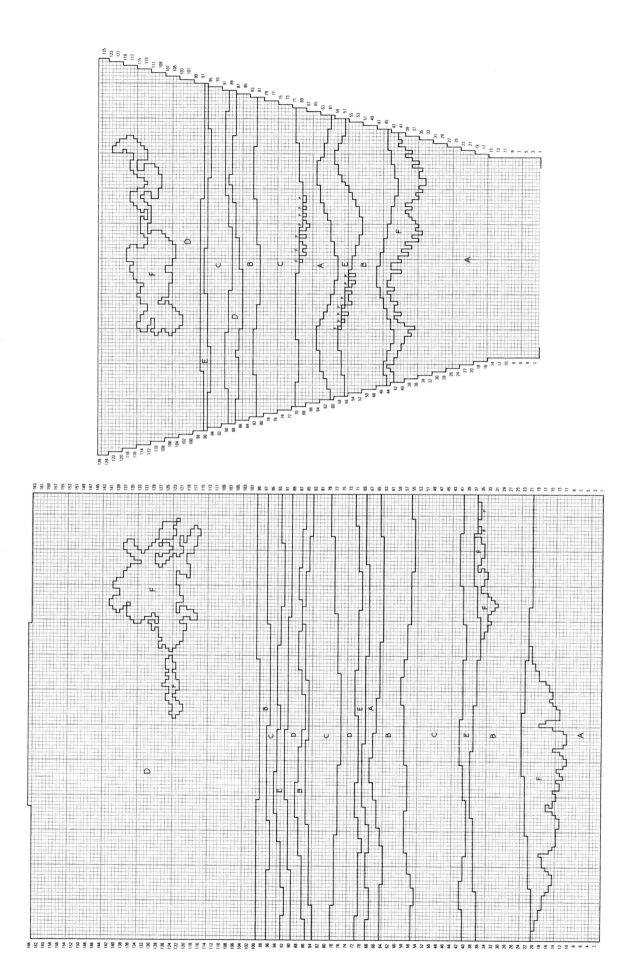

Right sleeve (the left sleeve is the same). For rib cast on 52sts and increase to 57sts on last row of rib.

Back 127sts Add rib

85

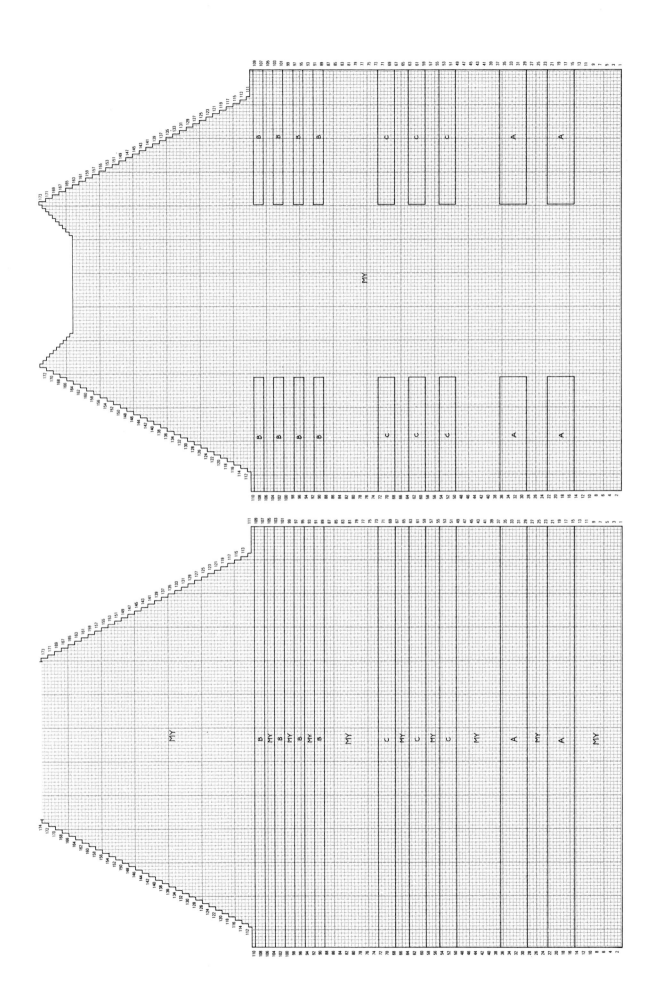

Front 125sts Add rib

Back 125sts Add rib

COLOUR BANDS

[See colour pages 50-51]

Traffic light colours contrast boldly with the black background of this man's jumper in double knitting. It is knitted in stocking stitch from a single rib, with raglan sleeves and a round neck.

Sizes to fit 101cm (40in) chest
Body length 47cm (18½in) to underarm including 9cm (2½in) single rib
Sleeve length 46cm (18in) to underarm including 9cm (2½in) single rib

Yarn Double Knitting 650g

MY Black	500g	**B** Yellow	50g
A Red	50g	**C** Green	50g

Needles 4mm (no.8) and 3¼ mm (no.10)

Tension 11 sts and 14 rows in st.st. on 4mm (no.8) needles over 5cm (2in) square.

Knit the sleeves as for **Camera** on page 66.

[See colour pages 52-53]

A subtle range of greys and black to simulate an animal's pelt. You could try a range of browns for a similar effect. Knitted in Chunky yarn in stocking stitch from a single rib, with dropped shoulders and a round neck.

Sizes to fit 86cm (34in) chest
Body length 38cm (15½in) to underarm including 7cm (3in) single rib
Sleeve length 44cm (17½in) to underarm including 7cm (3in) single rib.

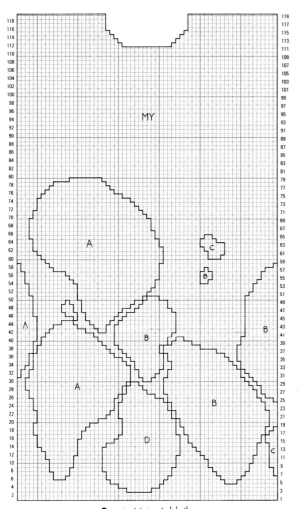

Front 64sts Add rib

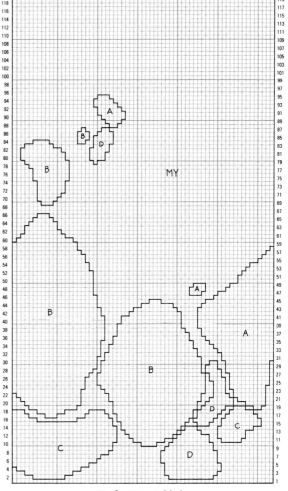

Back 64sts Add rib

87

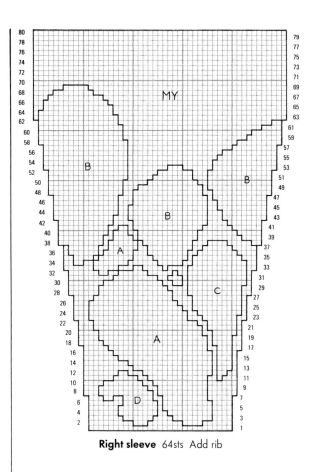

Right sleeve 64sts Add rib

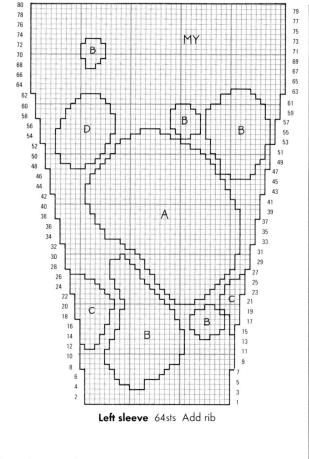

Left sleeve 64sts Add rib

Yarn Chunky 700g

MY Pale Grey	300g		**C** Fawn	100g
A Grey	100g		**D** Grey/Brown	100g
B Black	100g			

Needles 6½mm (no.3) and 5½mm (no.5)

Tension 7 sts and 10 rows in st.st. on 6½mm (no.3) needles to 5cm (2in) square.

Blue Mist

[See colour pages 54-55]

Pastel coloured mohair sweater knitted in stocking stitch in only two pieces from wrist to wrist, with garter stitch cuffs to turn back. Smaller flowers are embroidered on afterwards.

Body length to underarm 56cm (22in)
Sleeve length 41cm (16in) plus 7cm (3in) garter stitch cuff

Yarn Mohair type 450g

A Blue flecks	200g		**D** White flecks	100g
B Pale Blue	50g		**E** Grey	50g
C Mauve	50g			

Needles 4½mm (no.7) and 5½mm (no.5)

Tension 8 sts and 10 rows in st.st. on 5½mm (no.5) needles to 5cm (2in) square.

Knit sideways, starting at one cuff and finishing at the other.
When complete, pick up and knit garter stitch bands 1½in wide to attach round neck, cuffs and bottom edges.

Sizes to fit 86cm (34in) to 91cm (36in) chest

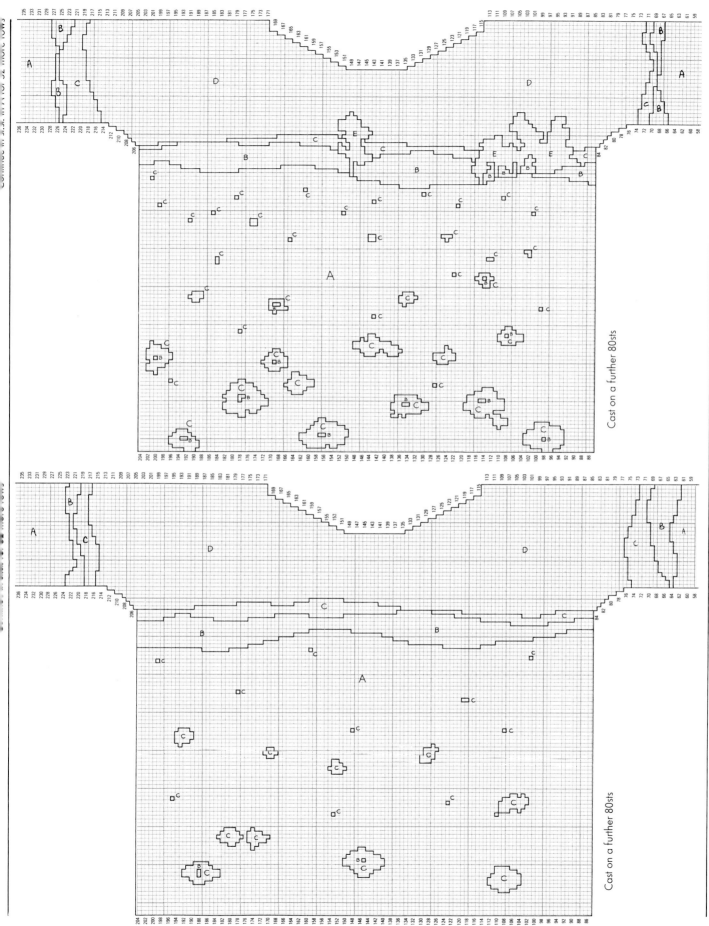

Front Cast on 27sts in A. Work 57 rows in st.st. then continue as chart.

Cast on a further 80sts

Back Cast on 27sts in A. Work 57 rows in st. st. then continue as chart

Cast on a further 80sts

89

CREATING YOUR OWN DESIGNS

There are two main processes involved in creating your own patterns. First of all you need to draw the outline of your chosen pattern shape (front, back and sleeves if any) onto squared paper. Then, inside the outline, you draw out your design in blocks showing where the different colours fall. You can then use the finished graph paper drawing to knit up the sweater in exactly the same way as knitting from the charts in this book (see instructions on page 56).

Before you begin you will need:

Several large sheets (32 x 22in) of graph paper divided into 1/10 inch squares
Plain paper for sketching
A soft pencil (2B)
Coloured pencils or paints
An eraser
Ruler
Set square

THE SWEATER SHAPE

Pick a pattern you like which has a simple style (either one of the ones on pages 103-6 or a pattern you have bought). One with set-in sleeves will be easier for matching a design across the seams than one with raglan sleeves, so avoid these unless the top part of your sweater will be plain. Any shaping instructions should be confined to the outside edges of the sweater pieces to avoid having to allow for increasing or decreasing within the design.

If you are planning on an intricate picture, choose a pattern using a fine yarn, with a high number of stitches and rows to the square inch. Thick yarns only work for big, bold designs.

CHECKING THE SIZE

Take a pencil and draw a ring round all the instructions in the pattern that apply to the size you want to knit (e.g. the numbers of stitches to be cast on, or decreased for armhole shapings, and back length measurements etc).

Check the measurements of the person you are knitting for by taking their underarm measurement, and their body length from the bottom edge of the sweater up to the armpit. If these measurements differ from the printed ones you can alter your chart to fit by adjusting the lengths on your charts as you construct it.

DRAWING THE FRONT

Take a large sheet of graph paper divided into one-tenth-of-an-inch squares. Mark the centre of the sheet of paper on the bottom line, and then draw the base line of your sweater front. It should stretch an equal distance either side of the centre point. For instance, if the pattern tells you to cast on 110 stitches, draw a line 110 squares long (11 inches), with 55 squares each side of the centre mark.

Count the number of rows there are in the pattern before you start the armhole shaping. Then draw a line upwards from each end of the base line for the correct number of squares to form the edges of the front. If the instructions give the number of rows to be worked, just count up the same number of squares to find the start of the armhole. If they give this information as a measurement you will need to calculate the number of rows from the tension information. Simply multiply the number of inches by the number of rows to the inch. For example, if you want to know how many rows there will be in 8 inches, and if the tension states that there are 7 rows to the inch, the number of rows will be 8 x 7 = 56.

At this point you can adjust the length of the sweater if you wish to by adding or subtracting the number of rows corresponding to the number of inches you want to alter it by.

Note on ribbing

As the ribbing is not usually part of the design, it need not be included in your chart. Don't forget to subtract the number of inches specified for the ribbing from your calculation of the length of the sides of your sweater, otherwise it will be too long.

Armhole shaping

Check the instructions for your pattern for armhole decreasing and draw a horizontal line inwards on each side for the number of squares equal to the number of stitches to be cast off. Continue for the rest of the armhole shaping, one row and one stitch still equalling one square.

Chest and neck

Finish the outline for the front in the same way, checking the pattern instructions and transferring them to your grid. Complete one side, then the other, following your pattern instructions for the neck shaping.

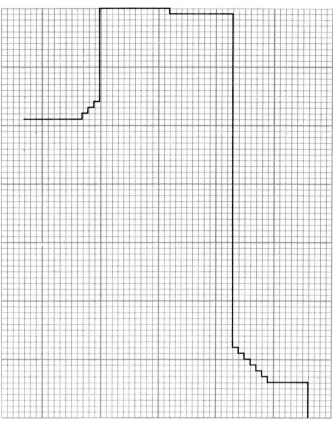

Drawing armhole and neck shapings onto the chart

DRAWING THE BACK AND SLEEVES

Make two more diagrams on graph paper from the instructions for the back and sleeve, including instructions for shaping and adjusting the lengths if necessary. If you are planning different designs for each sleeve you will need two sleeve outlines.

You have now prepared outline charts for each piece of your sweater in preparation for adding your design.

THE PICTURE DESIGN

STARTING WITH AN IDEA

Once you have decided to design your own picture knit, don't be put off if you feel you can't draw. You can start with a simple motif or design placed in the centre of the front or back of an otherwise plain sweater, which is much easier to do than an overall design which needs careful matching at the seams. An example of this approach is *Camera*.

If you don't want to use your imagination to create a new design you can look for an existing idea to copy or even trace. For instance, look through magazines, wallpaper sample books, library books on your favourite subject or sport, or go to a fabric shop and look at the designs on dress materials. The availability of such inspiration is infinite — just look around you for something you particularly like which is personal for you. This idea is also appropriate if you are knitting for someone else, which is how most of the sweaters in this book were begun. For example, the woolly sheep sweater (*Katie's Farm*) was knitted for Katie who lives on a farm, and it features her own sheepdog on the back. You can sketch your family pet or your house from family snapshots, just keeping the identifying features like your dog's one black ear. You won't need to put in very much detail for your design to be recognisable. The amount of detail that can be knitted is limited by the size of one knitted stitch. Anything smaller than that has to be embroidered on afterwards.

The amount of detail you can put on will also be affected by the thickness of yarn required for the pattern you have chosen. The finer the yarn the more detail you can include. 4-ply has more stitches to the tension square than double knitting yarn, so allows more intricate patterns, but the sweater will take you longer to knit, because of the fine yarn and small needle size. Double knitting yarn is the most useful for everyday wear, as it gives a reasonable amount of detail and a fairly quick result. Most of the sweaters in this book are in double knitting yarn. Double/double or chunky yarn is the quickest to knit because of the larger needle size required. However you can't get as much detail into a design for these yarns as there will be fewer stitches to the square inch. If you are using chunky yarn you should go for bold, dramatic results.

Geometric shapes are the easiest way to start, especially horizontal stripes or diagonal lines. Names or initials are also a good introduction to picture knitting as they have mostly straight lines. There is an alphabet chart on page 16 which you can use for lettering.

SKETCHING YOUR DESIGN

When you have decided what you will put on your sweater, make some preliminary sketches of the design in

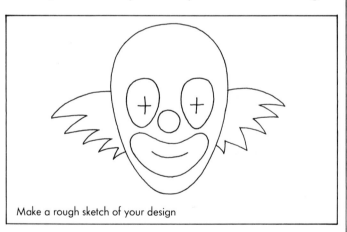

Make a rough sketch of your design

pencil on plain paper until you are happy with the result. Then draw a rough sweater shape on plain paper to look like the pattern you worked from in preparing the outline charts. The size of your sketch will depend on how much detail you want to include in your design.

Draw in your design where you want it to appear on the sweater shape, using a soft pencil so that you can easily rub out and change parts as necessary. A motif design is usually placed on the front of the sweater, either in the centre of the chest or on one side. But you could also place it at the bottom above the ribbing, or on the

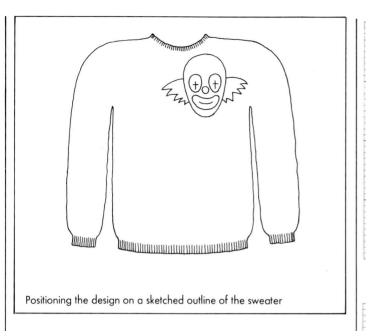

Positioning the design on a sketched outline of the sweater

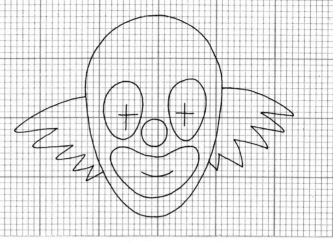

Drawing the sketch onto the graph paper

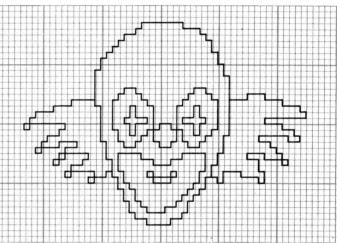

Squaring the drawing off following the grid

sleeve, or create an all-over pattern by repeating your motif. In order to look effective any motif should be at least 2 inches high on the sweater.

Then colour in the various blocks of the design with coloured pens, pencils or paints.

Do the same for the back of the sweater and the sleeves.

TRANSFERRING THE DESIGN ONTO YOUR CHART

Take your graph paper outline charts, and roughly sketch or trace on your design with a soft pencil. The size of the sketch will depend on the tension given for the thickness of yarn you will be using. For example, if you are using double knitting yarn and the pattern quotes a tension of 8 rows to one inch then a 2-inch high motif will have to be drawn as 2 x 8 rows (= 16 rows) high on the graph paper.

The limitations of the graph paper will show how much detail you can achieve on the knitted sweater as one square across equals one stitch and one square up or down equals one row.

When you are happy with this, carefully draw in the outlines of the blocks of colour, following the edges of the graph paper squares. Your sketch will probably include some curving lines. These have to be drawn as steps on the graph paper, but they will look quite like curves on the finished knitting, especially when viewed from a distance. Following the outline of your original drawing as closely as possible, draw round the angles of the graph paper squares to achieve an angular version of the original subject.

Draw in the final outlines of your design more firmly and rub out any rough outlines which are not wanted.

Do the same for each pattern shape — back, front and both sleeves (if each sleeve has a different design).

The stitch size problem

Graph paper squares represent stitches and rows but in reality stitches are not square. If you look at the tension instructions on a knitting pattern you will see that for an inch of knitting in depth there should be more stitches than for an inch of knitting in width. This is because a stitch is wider than it is high. A design on graph paper will therefore appear wider and shorter when it is knitted. So if you wish to allow for this you should draw your design on the graph paper looking slightly taller and thinner than you really want it to look. However, for most designs the finished result is a fair enough representation of the

93

original idea without making any allowance for this distortion.

If you do want to be really accurate, you can draw up your own grid paper with oblongs instead of squares to the exact size of stitch and row for the tension you want to achieve. This requires large sheets of plain paper, a set square for the corners and a ruler to draw all the lines. It does give a very accurate result for detailed knitting but it is a very time consuming method and not worthwhile for most sweaters.

Knitting a test motif

You can try out your design by choosing two or three colours of spare yarn to knit a test motif. Use the correct size of needles and type of yarn for the tension of your design and cast on enough stitches to allow for a border of plain knitting around it. Introduce new colours and change colours according to the methods described in the knitting techniques section. When you have finished your motif knit a few rows in the background colour before casting off. Then press your piece of knitting and compare it with your sketch.

DESIGNING IN THE ROUND

Patterns and pieces of knitting are flat and two-dimensional, but once made up into a garment and worn

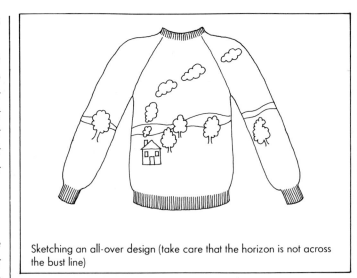

Sketching an all-over design (take care that the horizon is not across the bust line)

they become three-dimensional . When you are designing you must therefore consider the effect of the sweater in the round.

Always try to carry your design round to the back of the garment as this is much more effective than a picture which only appears on the front. You can also incorporate the sleeves into your design as they often look better made into part of the whole deisgn rather than left plain.

Consider the body shape of the person who will be wearing the sweater. For example, if she has rather wide hips it is more flattering to avoid too much detail around

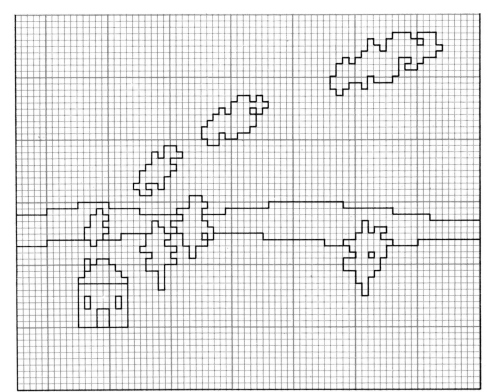

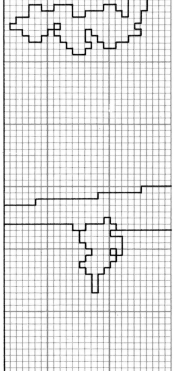

Make sure the picture matches up at the seams

the hipline and instead to concentrate on the upper part of the sweater. You can also consider making the sweater shorter, to just below the waist. Remember not to place details like clouds on a woman's sweater exactly on the bustline where they will be exaggerated in wear. Instead place them higher up near the shoulder. Always think about the body and how it moves while you are creating the design.

Joining the design at the seams

The main complication about designing 'in the round' is to make sure that the picture meets correctly at the seams. This is easy enough to do for a simple join like the front and back pieces, using the squares on the graph paper. Just count up the same number of rows from the bottom to find the same point on either side of the seam. Remember that the front and back are both viewed with the right side outside, so the left front joins the left back and the right front joins the right back.

Check every join in your design in this way to make sure they meet correctly everywhere. Look at some of the charts at the front of this book such as *Autumn Stripes* to see how these designs have been matched up at the seams.

Joining rows to stitches

In some places on the sweater (e.g. where the sleeve top joins the front or back) the design may have to match up a section of vertical knitting (rows) with a section of horizontal knitting (stitches). The measurement of the two areas will be different because a stitch is wider than it is high, so a calculation must be made based on the tension instructions for the sweater, which will show you whether the stitch is a lot wider than it is high or only slightly so. This calculation only needs to be done roughly as the two sections can usually be made to fit together when you are sewing up the seams, by stretching one of the seams slightly to fit.

You will be able to see by looking at your charts where

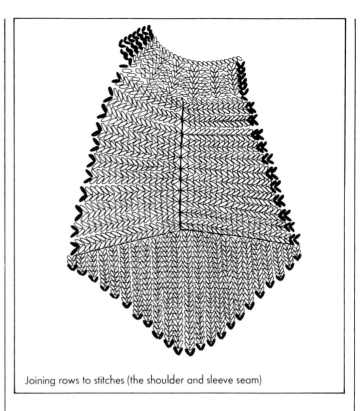

Joining rows to stitches (the shoulder and sleeve seam)

the centre of the sleeve top is, and this is the point which will join up with the top edge of the armhole shaping on the front and back pieces. The sleeve edge will join up with the bottom edge of the armhole shaping, and from this you will be able to judge with reasonable accuracy how the picture design will carry over from one piece to the next.

ADDING THE KEY

Mark the desired colour for each block of your design either using coloured pencils, or a key system such as the initial letter of each colour. Unless you have designed it with specific colours of yarn in mind this will be only a rough guide, as you may find that the colour scheme will have to be adapted slightly to fit in with the shade ranges available in the type of yarn you want to use.

BUYING YARN

COLOURS

You can either look for yarn colours in the shops which nearly match the ideas in your sketch, or look at yarns first and design your sweater with specific colours in mind. You may not be able to buy exactly the colours you had in mind, unless they are basic or primary tones. There is generally a wider choice of colours in the knitting department of large department stores than in smaller local shops. Some firms supply yarn by post, which you can choose from a catalogue of sample swatches. This is a good idea if your local wool shop has only a limited range of colours and if you remember to order in advance – it can be frustrating to have your design ready and be waiting for the yarn to arrive.

THICKNESS OF YARN

Always choose yarn of the type stated in the pattern on which you based your chart. If you change the thickness of yarn you will also have to check your tension and change the size of the needles to be used in order to achieve the same size of sweater. You will find if you have chosen double-double or chunky yarn that your choice of colours may be more limited as they tend to be sold only in a narrow range of primary colours and basics like black and navy blue. For example the chunky wool used for *Animal Skin* comes in a small range of black and greys which are particularly appropriate for this design.

WOOL OR SYNTHETIC?

Yarns are made of pure wool, synthetics like nylon, or a mixture of both.

Pure wool
Many designers prefer pure wool for its 'feel' and the fact that it keeps its shape better than a synthetic yarn, so it is a good choice for the basic background colour of your design, and for the ribbing. It can be used in conjunction with synthetics for the details of the design, so long as the same thickness is chosen. Pure wool usually needs hand-washing – look at the instructions on the ball-band.

Synthetics
There is a wider choice of colour and special effects like lurex in synthetic yarns, and they are also generally cheaper than pure wool. They tend to stretch out of shape more easily than wool, which is more elastic. They can usually be machine washed.

Mixtures
A mixture of wool and synthetic is a good compromise in terms of cost and durability. One with a higher proportion of wool than synthetic is recommended for picture knitting.

Yarns for special effects
Small quantities of different plys or textures can be used for special effects (for instance mohair for fluffy clouds or animals). They should be used with two or three strands together if they are much thinner than the main yarn. You may already have oddments of yarn left from previous sweaters – it is a good idea to keep a bag of such oddments as they are useful for small details in picture knitting. Some examples of the use of yarns for special effects in this book are the fence in *Katie's Farm* which was knitted in white dishcloth cotton for a firm, smooth contrast to the fluffier main yarn, and the sheep in the same sweater, which were knitted in cream Aran wool to simulate their woolly coats. Shetland wool was used for *Yorkshire Moors* for a suitably muted, misty effect.

CALCULATING YARN QUANTITIES

The total amount of yarn needed for your sweater will be shown in the pattern on which you based your chart. Remember to adjust this amount if you significantly lengthened or shortened the sweater. If you are knitting in several colours you will then need to work out how much of each colour to buy.

First, estimate how much of the sweater is in the main yarn. For example, the background colour may be about 50 per cent of the total area of the sweater. Make a similar estimate for each different colour area, adjusting them so that the total of your percentages adds up to 100. So, for example, as well as the 50 per cent in the main colour, you might reckon that about 25 per cent was in the second colour, 15 per cent in the third colour and 10 per cent in the fourth.

The next thing to do is to divide up the total weight of yarn needed for the sweater between the different colours. For example, if the total quantity of yarn needed is 500g and the main colour is 50 per cent of the total area you will need 250g of the main colour, and so on.

Finally you can work out how many balls of each colour to buy according to the weight of ball in which your chosen yarn is sold. For example if one colour is sold in 50g balls and you need 125g altogether you will have to buy 3 balls (150g) to cover the necessary amount.

You can see that the more colours you choose to use in your sweater the more yarn you will have to buy to make sure you have enough (for example the above calculation shows you will buy 25g more than you need of one colour). To avoid too much waste either restrict the number of colours you choose to two or three or choose a yarn which is sold in smaller ball weights like 20g or 25g, rather than 50g.

You can also work this calculation process the other way round: If the total required is 500g you cannot use more than 10 different colours (in roughly equal areas) without some wastage of yarn. This is useful if you have a particular yarn in mind and want to design around it.

Length/weight

Yarn is sold by weight of ball, not the length of yarn in each ball. Calculations on the amount to buy will therefore always be approximate, because yarns of the same weight may have a different length and any variations of tension or fancy stitches will use up different amounts. When you have knitted several picture sweaters you will begin to build up a stock of left-over yarns which are useful for knitting the smaller details in your next sweater. You will also begin to get a feel for the size of the area you can knit with different amounts of yarn, which is a useful skill for picture knitting which you can only acquire with practice.

Buy more, not less

If you are still in doubt about how much yarn to buy it's a good idea to buy a little more than you think you will need. If you skimp on the yarn and run out before the sweater is complete, the next batch of yarn in the shop may have a different dye number and be a slightly different colour (or worse, the shop may have sold out of your yarn altogether!). A different dye number would probably not matter for detailed picture knitting where a slightly different colour will be less noticeable, but it could show on a large area of background colour, such as halfway up a sleeve. If this happens it's probably better to reknit the whole sleeve with the new dye number yarn.

Some woolshops will refund your money if you return a whole ball, complete with its ball-band, with the receipt from your original purchase. So remember to keep your receipt in a safe place — it could be useful. Some shops only give refunds if they still have your particular dye number in stock, so if you want to do this go back to the shop with the surplus yarn as soon as possible after finishing your sweater. This is a useful economy measure if you have chosen a particularly expensive brand of yarn. Cheaper yarns can go into your stock for the next sweater, giving more choice of colour in the future.

Some woolshops will reserve yarn so that you do not have to buy the total amount all at once. There is usually a time limit on this 'putting by' service, after which they will return your yarn to the shelves, so check this when you make the reservation. A typical time limit is two months.

USING FLUFFY AND TEXTURED YARNS

There are various unusual or special yarns available which can be used for different effects on picture sweaters.

Fluffy yarns

Pure mohair is the best known fluffy yarn but it is quite expensive. However, there are many synthetic fluffy yarns available which make good substitutes for mohair. Fluffy baby yarns are good for small areas like clouds because they are sold in smaller balls of 20g or 25g. (Fluffy baby yarn was used for the clouds on *Katie's Farm*). These yarns can also be used for animals, such as the embroidered monkey on *Palm Trees*. You can even knit a whole sweater in mohair-type yarn if you want a misty effect, but less detail is possible with this sort of yarn because the edges of the colour blocks are blurred by the fluffy texture, so a simple design would be best.

If your chosen fluffy yarn is much finer than the main yarn, knit it with two strands together for extra bulk.

Textured yarns

Textured yarns are useful for special effects, and have been used in various ways for the sweaters in this book. *Palm Trees* has a rough, scratchy yarn for the bark of the trees. *Animal Skin* has a rough, coarse chunky wool for the whole sweater, for the animal pelt effect. *Katie's Farm* has cream Aran wool for the sheep and dishcloth cotton for the fence. *Yorkshire Moors* is knitted in muted shades of Shetland wool for a misty effect.

These are just some examples of the use of textured yarns. Look at the wide range available and you're sure to find inspiration. Lurex yarn is especially good for adding sparkle to evening sweaters. You can try winding lurex thread around your main yarn to knit with the two twisted together.

SPECIAL EFFECTS

Once you have designed a basic picture knit there are many ways to enhance it to make it even more interesting and individual. These fall into three main categories. You can experiment with different stitches to give varying textures to the sweater, use embroidery stitches to put on more detail, or sew on extra trimmings for amusing or unusual effects. The examples given here are based on those used for the sweaters at the front of the book, and should inspire you to think of some new ideas of your own.

STITCHES TO GIVE TEXTURE

You can use different knitting stitches to give patterns and textures to specific areas of your design.

Purl
This is a good stitch for adding a raised or lumpy look to parts of otherwise plain stocking stitch areas. It is particularly effective to make trees or clouds stand out from their backgrounds, for example the trees on *Balloon* and *Yorkshire Moors*.

The first stitch after the colour change should still be in stocking stitch. (If you purl it on the right side you will get a stitch which is half in the first colour and half in the second). This will form a frame of stocking stitch around the raised area of purl.

Moss stitch
This is one stitch knitted and the next purled, alternated on the next row.
It can also be used for trees. For example the deciduous trees on *Katie's Farm* are in moss stitch, to contrast with the coniferous trees in stocking stitch.

Random moss stitch
This is not as regular as ordinary moss stitch. Here the knit and purl stitches are placed at random for an even more irregular effect, such as on the sheep on *Katie's Farm*.

Stepped ribbing
This was used on *Yorkshire Moors* to give the effect of the narrow stones which are used on top of dry-stone walls. The ribbing was knitted to various heights with stocking stitch showing between to indicate the fields which can be seen through the wall.

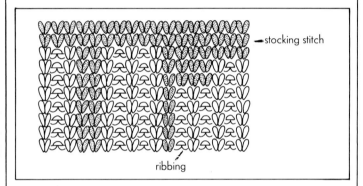

Representative effect
Stitches can also be used to represent fabrics or garments. For example the fishnet stockings on *Leopardskin Rug* are knitted with alternate black and pink stitches to represent the effect of fishnet stockings on pink legs.

Another example is the use of two colours knitted diagonally to represent ploughed fields, which is used on the front of *Oak Tree*. This is knitted with two stitches in the background colour then one stitch in contrast on each row, repeated in steps to give a diagonal effect.

EMBROIDERY

There are several embroidery stitches which can be used for adding detail and decorations to finished sweaters. Remember to keep your stitches smooth to avoid puckering the knitting.

Swiss darning
This covers the basic knitted stitch with another colour, so they form a guide for the embroidery stitch. It can be worked horizontally and vertically.

Swiss darning

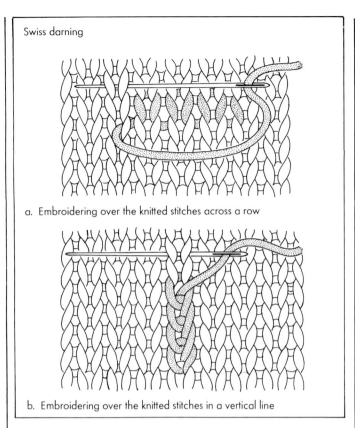

a. Embroidering over the knitted stitches across a row

b. Embroidering over the knitted stitches in a vertical line

Swiss darning was added to several of the sweaters in this book, for example *Bike* and *Star Wars*.

Back stitch

This is the easiest way to add long lines, whether straight or curving. It helps to mark the piece of knitting with pins or chalk as a guide for the embroidery stitches.

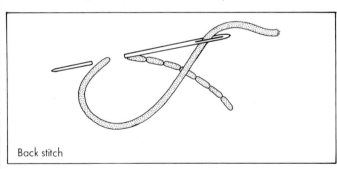

Back stitch

Back stitch was used for the facial features of *Woman* and *Leopardskin Rug*, for the name on the boat and plane and the face of the clock in *Cityscape*, and for many details on *Star Wars*, where it was sometimes worked between the vertical lines of stitches for a more subtle effect.

French knot

This is useful for small spots like flower centres and animals' eyes.

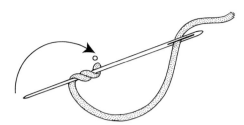

French knot
Wrap the thread round the needle a few times before putting the needle back into its original hole

It was used for the flower centres on the front of *Oak Tree*, where some of the flowers were worked on the ribbing for a more unusual effect.

French knots were also used for the starry sky on *Star Wars*.

Satin stitch

This stitch is used for covering larger areas of embroidery and produces a raised or padded effect.

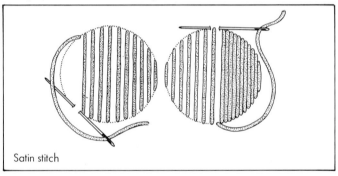

Satin stitch

It was used for the lips of the women on *Leopardskin Rug* and *Woman* and for the heads of the sheep on *Katie's Farm*.

Cross stitch

This can be completed one stitch at a time or by making

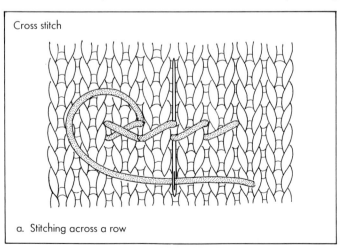

Cross stitch

a. Stitching across a row

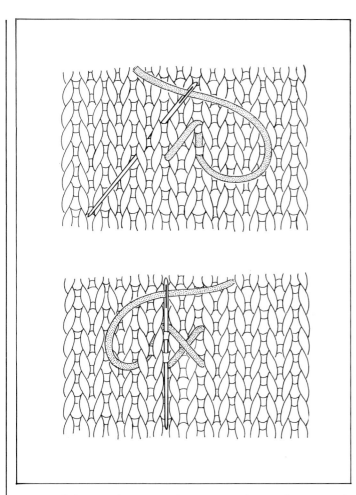

a row of diagonals in one direction and completing each cross on the return row.

Chain stitch

Chain stitch can be worked in a line to form curves, or used singly or in circles for leaf or petal shapes.

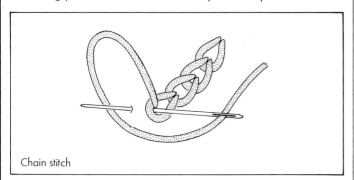

Chain stitch

Embroidered pictures

A very quick method of creating a picture knit was used for the *Sportsmen* sweaters. The sweater is knitted in stocking stitch with just a single row of contrasting colour to represent the pitch. The figures are then embroidered

on afterwards. This makes a sweater which can be worn by anyone who is reluctant to wear an all-over picture knit. If it is worn under a jacket the sporting figures are covered and the sweater appears to be totally plain. Remove the jacket and the scene is revealed! This concept could be used for any little scene or similar small motif such as initials or a name.

If you are not sure about embroidering straight onto your sweater, make a drawing first (see p.77). Tack the piece of paper onto the sweater, embroider over it to fill in the shapes and then undo the tacking and pull away all the unwanted paper.

Leave tacking until embroidery is finished

Embroidering over a paper sketch

Trimmings

There are many trimmings available in craft or needlework shops. They must be attached securely to the knitting and must be washable – unless you are prepared to have your picture sweater dry cleaned.

Animal features

Craft shops sell eyes and noses which are meant for toymaking. These can look very effective on a sweater as they stick out from the surface of the knitting (as on *Leopardskin Rug*).

You can also sew on pieces of felt to form ears or a tongue. Thick thread makes good hanging whiskers, especially with knots at the base.

Lace and ribbon

These are particularly effective when used to trim knitted underwear as on *Woman*.

Buttons

You can sew real buttons onto a sweater without an

opening for a trompe l'oeil effect, or use them for eyes. Knitted stockings can have a button sewn on to imitate suspenders.

Pom-poms

These can be made from scraps of wool for added decoration, as for the shoes on *Leopardskin Rug*.

Sequins

For a sparkly effect, sequins can be sewn onto a sweater, at random or in lines and patterns. Make sure they are securely attached by threading the needle through the hole in each sequin and securing it with backstitch.

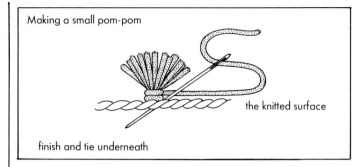

Making a small pom-pom

the knitted surface

finish and tie underneath

BASIC PATTERNS

PATTERNS USING DOUBLE KNITTING YARN

To fit 51 **56** 61 **66** 71 **76** 81 **86** 91 **96** 101 **107** 112 **117** cm chest (20 **22** 24 **26** 28 **30** 32 **34** 36 **38** 40 **42** 44 **46** in)

Actual size 56 **61** 66 **71** 76 **81** 86 **91** 96 **101** 107 **112** 117 **122** cm (22 **24** 26 **28** 30 **32** 34 **36** 38 **40** 42 **44** 46 **48** in)

Length 30 **34** 38 **42** 46 **50** 53 **61** 66 **69** 69 **69** 71 **71** cm (12 **13½** 15 **16½** 18 **19½** 21 **24** 24 **24** 24 **24** 27 **27** in)

Side seam 15 **17** 20 **27** 29 **32** 37 **38** 38 **38** 41 **41** 41 **41** cm (6 **6½** 8 **10½** 11½ **12½** 14½ **15** 15 **15** 16 **16** 16 **16** in)

Sleeve seam 18 **22** 25 **29** 33 **38** 41 **43** 43 **46** 48 **48** 48 **48** cm (7 **8½** 10 **11½** 13 **15** 16 **17** 17 **18** 19 **19** 19 **19** in)

Needles 4mm (no.8) and 3¼ mm (no.10)

Tension 12 sts and 16 rows to 5cm (2in) square on 4mm (no.8) needles

Back (all designs)

Using 3¼ mm (no.10) ndls cast on 67 **73** 79 **85** 91 **97** 103 **109** 115 **121** 127 **133** 139 **145** sts.

Work 4 **6** 8 **8** 8 **8** 8 **8** 8 **8** 8 **8** 8 **8** cm (1½ **2** 3 **3** 3 **3** 3 **3** 3 **3** 3 **3** 3 **3** in) k1,p1 rib.

Change to 4mm (no.8) ndls. Beg. k,cont in st.st. until work measures 15 **17** 20 **27** 29 **32** 37 **38** 38 **38** 41 **41** 41 **41** cm (6 **6½** 8 **10½** 11½ **12½** 14½ **15** 15 **15** 15 **16** 16 **16** in), ending p.

Shape armholes Cast off 3 **3** 3 **4** 4 **4** 5 **5** 5 **5** 5 **5** 6 **6** sts at beg of next 2 rows (61 **67** 73 **77** 83 **91** 93 **99** 105 **111** 117 **123** 127 **133** sts)*

Work 4 **4** 5 **5** 6 **6** 7 **10** 11 **14** 15 **18** 18 **19** rows dec once at each end of every row (53 **59** 63 **67** 71 **79** 79 **79** 83 **83** 87 **87** 91 **95** sts)**

Cont without shaping until armholes measures 15 **17** 18 **15** 17 **18** 16 **23** 23 **23** 20 **20** 28 **28** cm (6 **7** 7 **6** 6½ **7** 6½ **9** 9 **9** 8 **8** 11 **11** in), ending p.

Shape shoulders Cast off 8 **8** 8 **10** 10 **10** 11 **11** 12 **12** 12 **12** 14 **14** sts at beg of next 4 rows (21 **27** 31 **27** 31 **39** 35 **35** 35 **35** 39 **39** 35 **35** sts).

Cast off rem sts for V neck or break off yarn and slip these sts on thread or stitch holder for round or polo neck.

Sleeves

Using 3¼ mm (no.10) ndls cast on 28 **30** 32 **35** 38 **41** 45 **49** 51 **57** 61 **65** 67 **67** sts.

Work 4 **6** 8 **8** 8 **8** 8 **8** 8 **8** 8 **8** 8 **8** cm (1½ **2** 3 **3** 3 **3** 3 **3** 3 **3** 3 **3** 3 **3** in) k1,p1 rib.

Change to 4mm (no.8) ndls.

Beg k, cont in st.st, increasing one st at each end of 5th and every fol 5th **5th** 4th **4th** 4th **5th** 5th **5th** 7th **8th** 9th **10th** 10th **10th** row until

44 **50** 56 **62** 68 **74** 80 **86** 89 **89** 91 **91** 91 **95** sts.

Cont straight until work measures 18 **22** 25 **29** 33 **38** 41 **43** 43 **46** 48 **48** 48 **48** cm (7 **8½** 10 **11½** 13 **15** 16 **17** 17 **18** 19 **19** 19 **19** in), ending p.

Cast off 1 st at beg of next 30 **35** 38 **40** 40 **40** 48 **48** 48 **50** 50 **50** 52 **52** rows.

Cast off 2 sts at beg of next 2 **2** 4 **4** 4 **6** 10 **8** 10 **10** 10 **10** 10 **12** rows.

Cast of rem 10 **11** 10 **14** 20 **22** 22 **22** 21 **19** 19 **19** 19 **19** sts.

Front (round and polo neck designs)

Work exactly as given for back to**

Cont without shaping until armhole measures 8 **10** 10 **8** 9 **10** 9 **15** 15 **15** 13 **13** 20 **20** cm (3 **4** 4 **3** 3½ **4** 3½ **6** 6 **6** 5 **5** 8 **8** in), ending p.

Next row s1, k19 **22** 23 **25** 32 **31** 30 **30** 32 **32** 34 **34** 35 **37**, turn.

Working on these 20 **23** 24 **26** 33 **32** 31 **31** 33 **33** 35 **35** 36 **38** sts only, cont as follows:

Next row Dec 1, p to end.

Work 3 **6** 7 **5** 12 **11** 8 **8** 8 **8** 10 **10** 11 **9** row dec once at neck edge on every row (16 **16** 16 **20** 20 **20** 22 **22** 24 **24** 24 **24** 28 **28** sts).

Cont without shaping until armhole measures same as back, ending p.

Shape shoulder Cast off 8 **8** 8 **10** 10 **10** 11 **11** 12 **12** 12 **12** 14 **14** sts.

Next row, p.

Cast of rem 8 **8** 8 **10** 10 **10** 11 **11** 12 **12** 12 **12** 14 **14** sts.

With right side facing, slip first 13 **13** 15 **15** 15 **15** 15 **17** 17 **17** 17 **17** 19 **19** sts onto a thread or stitch-holder. Rejoin yarn to rem 20 **23** 24 **26** 33 **32** 31 **31** 33 **33** 35 **35** 36 **38** sts and proceed as follows:

Next row k to end.

Next row p to last 2 sts, p 2 tog.

Work 3 **6** 7 **5** 12 **11** 8 **8** 8 **8** 10 **10** 11 **9** rows dec once at neck edge on every row (16 **16** 16 **20** 20 **20** 22 **22** 24 **24** 24 **24** 28 **28** sts).

Cont without shaping until armhole measures same as back, ending k.

Shape shoulder Cast off 8 **8** 8 **10** 10 **10** 11 **11** 12 **12** 12 **12** 14 **14** sts, p to end.

Next row k.

Cast off rem 8 **8** 8 **10** 10 **10** 11 **11** 12 **12** 12 **12** 14 **14** sts.

Neckband and polo neck

Join right shoulder seam.

With right side facing, using 3¼ mm (no.10) ndls, beg at top of left

shoulder. Pick up and knit 8 **10** 12 **14** 16 **18** 20 **21** 24 **24** 22 **22** 23 **23** sts along left side of neck.
Knit up 13 **13** 15 **15** 15 **15** 15 **17** 17 **17** 17 **17** 19 **19** sts left at front of neck.
Pick up and knit 8 **10** 12 **14** 16 **18** 20 **21** 24 **24** 22 **22** 23 **23** sts along right side of neck and pick up or knit across 21 **27** 31 **27** 31 **39** 35 **35** 35 **35** 39 **39** 35 **35** sts left at back of neck (50 **60** 70 **70** 74 **90** 95 **94** 100 **100** 100 **100** 100 **100** sts).
Neckband Work 3 **3** 3 **3** 3 **3** 4 **4** 4 **4** 4 **4** 5 **5** cm (1 **1** 1 **1** 1 **1** 1½ **1½** 1½ **1½** 1½ **1½** 2 **2** in) single rib.
Cast off loosely in rib.
Polo neck Work 10 **10** 10 **13** 13 **13** 15 **15** 15 **15** 15 **15** 18 **18** cm (4 **4** 4 **5** 5 **5** 6 **6** 6 **6** 6 **6** 7 **7** in) single rib.
Cast off loosely in rib.

Front (V neck design)

Work as for back to *
Knit 30 **33** 36 **38** 41 **45** 46 **49** 52 **55** 58 **61** 63 **66**, k 2 tog, turn.
Work 4 **4** 5 **5** 6 **6** 7 **10** 11 **14** 15 **18** 18 **19** rows dec 1 st at armhole edge on every row. At the same time dec 1 st at neck edge on next and every fol 4th **4th** 3rd **3rd** 3rd **2nd** 2nd **4th** 4th **4th** 3rd **3rd** 5th **4th** row.
Work 44 **52** 51 **43** 46 **50** 45 **62** 61 **58** 49 **46** 70 **69** rows cont dec once at neck edge only in 4th **4th** 3rd **3rd** 3rd **2nd** 2nd **4th** 4th **4th** 3rd **3rd** 5th **4th** row (16 **16** 16 **20** 20 **20** 22 **22** 24 **24** 24 **24** 28 **28** sts), ending p.
Cast off 8 **8** 8 **10** 10 **10** 11 **11** 12 **12** 12 **12** 14 **14** sts, k to end.
Next row p.
Cast of rem 8 **8** 8 **10** 10 **10** 11 **11** 12 **12** 12 **12** 14 **14** sts.
With right side facing, rejoin yarn to rem 30 **33** 36 **38** 41 **45** 46 **49** 52 **55** 58 **61** 63 **66** sts and complete right side to match left, reversing all shapings.
Neckband for V neck
Join right shoulder seam.
With right side facing, using 3¼ mm (no.10) ndls, beg at top of left shoulder. Pick up and knit 35 **39** 39 **43** 43 **43** 47 **47** 47 **51** 51 **51** 55 **55** sts evenly along left side of neck, pick up loop at centre of V and k into back of it, pick up and knit 35 **39** 39 **43** 43 **43** 47 **47** 47 **51** 51 **51** 55 **55** sts evenly along right side of neck and pick up and knit 21 **27** 31 **27** 31 **39** 35 **35** 35 **35** 39 **39** 35 **35** sts along back of neck (92 **106** 110 **114** 118 **126** 130 **130** 130 **138** 138 **138** 146 **146** sts).
Mark centre st of V with a coloured thread.
1st row s1 *p1, k1, rep from * to end.
2nd row Rib to 2 sts before marked st, k 2 tog tbl, k1, k2 tog, rib to end.
3rd row Rib to 2 sts before marked st, p2 tog, p1, p2 tog tbl, rib to end.
Rep last 2 rows twice more.
Cast off in rib.

To make up
Sew up left shoulder and neckband seams. Set in sleeves, then sew up side and sleeve seams.

Armhole edge for sleeveless sweater

Sew up left shoulder seam.
With right side facing using 3¼ mm (no.10) ndls, pick up and knit 58 **64** 70 **76** 82 **88** 94 **100** 122 **130** 136 **144** 144 **152** sts evenly all round armhole edge.
Work 8 rows single rib.
Cast off loosely in rib.

To make up sleeveless sweater
Sew up side seams.

PATTERNS USING CHUNKY YARN

To fit 81 **86** 91 **96** 101 **107** 112 cm chest (32 **34** 36 **38** 40 **42** 44 in)
For measurements see patterns with double knitting yarn.

Needles 5½mm (no.5) and 6½mm (no.3).
Tension 7 sts and 10 rows to 5cm (2in) square on 6½mm (no.3)

Back (all designs)

Using 5½mm (no.5) ndls cast on 57 **59** 63 **67** 71 **73** 77 sts.
Work 7.5cm (3in) k1,p1 rib.
Change to 6½mm (no.3) ndls and st.st.
Cont in st.st. until work measures 37 **38** 38 **38** 41 **41** 41 cm (14½ **15** 15 **15** 16 **16** 16 in), ending p.
Shape armholes Cast off 3 sts at beg of next 2 rows (51 **53** 57 **61** 65 **67** 71 sts)
Work 5 **6** 7 **9** 10 **11** 12 rows dec once at each end of every row (41 **41** 43 **43** 45 **45** 47 sts)* *
Cont without shaping until armhole measures 17 **23** 23 **23** 20 **20** 28 cm (6½ **9** 9 **9** 8 **8** 11 in), ending p.
Shape shoulders Cast off 6 **6** 6 **6** 7 **7** 7 sts at beg of next 2 rows.
Cast of 7 **7** 7 **7** 7 **7** 7 sts at beg of next 2 rows.
Cast off rem 15 **15** 17 **17** 17 **17** 19 sts for V neck, or break off yarn and slip these sts on thread or stitch holder for round or polo neck.

Front (round and polo neck designs)

Work as for back to * *
Cont without shaping until armhole measures 9 **15** 15 **15** 13 **13** 20 cm (3 **6** 6 **6** 5 **5** 8 in), ending p.
Shape neck
Next row s1, k16 **16** 17 **17** 18 **18** 19 sts, turn.
Working on these 17 **17** 18 **18** 19 **19** 20 sts only, proceed as follows:
Next row s1, p to last st, k1.
Work 4 **4** 5 **5** 5 **5** 6 rows dec once at neck edge only on every row (13 **13** 13 **13** 14 **14** 15 sts).
Cont without shaping until armhole measures same as the back, ending p.
Shape shoulder
Next row Cast off 6 **6** 6 **6** 7 **7** 8 sts, k to end.
Next row s1, p to end.
Cast off rem 7 **7** 7 **7** 7 **7** 7 sts.
With right side facing, slip first 7 sts of rem 24 **24** 25 **25** 26 **26** 27 sts onto a thread or stitch holder, rejoin yarn to rem 17 **17** 18 **18** 19 **19**

20 sts and complete to match left side, reversing all shapings.
Sew up right shoulder seam.

Neckband (round and polo neck designs)

Using 5½mm (no.5) ndls, with right side facing, begin at top of left shoulder, pick up and knit 15 sts evenly along left side of neck, knit across 7 sts left at front of neck, pick up and knit 16 sts evenly along right side of neck and knit across 15 **15** 17 **17** 17 **17** 19 sts left at back of neck (53 **53** 55 **55** 55 **55** 57 sts).

Round neck
Work 5 rows k1,p1 rib.
Cast off loosely in rib.

Polo neck
Work 15 **15** 15 **15** 15 **15** 15 cm (6 **6** 6 **6** 6 **6** 6 in) k1,p1 rib.
Cast off loosely in rib.

Sleeves

Using 5½mm (no.5) ndls cast on 29 **31** 31 **31** 33 **33** 35 sts.
Work 16 rows k1,p1 rib.
Change to 6½mm (no.3) ndls and cont in st.st inc once at each end of 3rd and every fol 8th row to 43 **45** 45 **45** 47 **47** 49 sts.
Cont without shaping until work measures 41 **43** 43 **46** 48 **48** 48 cm (16 **17** 17 **18** 19 **19** 19 in), ending p.
Shape top
Dec 1 st at beg of next 16 **18** 18 **18** 20 **20** 22 rows.
Cast off 2 sts at beg of next 6 **6** 6 **6** 6 **6** 6 rows.
Cast off rem 15 sts.

Front (V neck design)

Work as for back until work is 6 rows less than back to armhole.
Next row sl, k27 **28** 30 **32** 34 **35** 37, turn.
Working on these 28 **29** 31 **33** 35 **36** 38 sts only, proceed as follows:
Next row sl, p to last st, k1.
Work 4 rows dec once at neck edge in 1st row (27 **28** 30 **32** 34 **35** 36 sts).
Shape armhole Cast off 3 sts, k to last 2 sts, k2 tog.
Next row sl, p to last st, k1.
Work 5 **6** 7 **9** 10 **11** 12 rows dec once at armhole edge in every row and at same time dec once at neck edge in 3rd and every fol 4th row (17 **17** 17 **17** 18 **17** 17 sts).
Work 9 **4** 17 **15** 14 **13** 13 rows dec once at neck edge only in 2nd **1st** 4th **2nd** 1st **4th** 4th and every fol 4th row (15 **16** 13 **13** 14 **14** 14 sts).
For first 2 sizes (81 and 86cm) Work 8/14 rows dec once at neck edge only in next and every fol 6th row (13 sts).
For all sizes Cont without shaping until armhole measures same as back, ending p.
Shape shoulder Cast off 6 **6** 6 **6** 7 **7** 7 sts, k to end.
Cast off rem 7 sts.
With right side facing, slip 1st of rem 29 **30** 32 **34** 36 **37** 39 sts on a thread or safety pin, rejoin yarn to rem 28 **29** 31 **33** 35 **36** 38 sts and complete to match left side, reversing all shapings.

Neckband (V neck design)

Using 5½mm (no.5) ndls, with right side facing, begin at top of left shoulder, pick up and knit 29 **31** 31 **31** 33 **33** 33 sts evenly along left side of neck, knit st from centre of V left on thread, pick up and knit 30 **32** 32 **32** 34 **34** 34 sts evenly along right side of neck and 15 **15** 17 **17** 17 **17** 17 sts from back of neck (75 **79** 81 **81** 85 **85** 85 sts).

1st row sl1, *p1,k1, rep from * to end.
2nd row rib to 2 sts from marked st, k 2 tog tbl, k1, k 2 tog, rib to end.
3rd row Rib to 2 sts from marked st, p 2 tog, p1, p 2 tog tbl, rib to end.
Rep last 2 rows once.
Cast off in rib.

To make up
Sew left shoulder and neckband seam.
Set in sleeves.
Join side and underarm seams.

PATTERNS USING 4-PLY YARN

To fit 51 **56** 61 **66** 71 **76** 81 **86** 91 **96** cm chest (20 **22** 24 **26** 28 **30** 32 34 36 38 in).
For measurements see patterns with double knitting yarn.
Needles 3¼mm (no.10) and 2¾mm (no. 12).
Tension 14 sts and 18 rows to 5cm (2in) square on 3¼mm (no.10) ndls.

Back (all designs)

Using 2¾mm (no.12) ndls, cast on 77 **87** 91 **97** 105 **111** 119 **125** 133 **140** sts and work 4 **6** 8 **8** 8 **8** 8 **8** 8 cm (1½ **2** 3 **3** 3 **3** 3 **3** 3 in) k1, p1 rib.
Change to 3¼mm (no.10) ndls and cont in st.st until work measures 15 **17** 20 **27** 29 **32** 37 **38** 38 **38** cm (6 **6½** 8 **10½** 11½ **12½** 14½ **15** 15 **15** in), ending p.
Shape armholes Cast off 3 **7** 7 **7** 7 **7** 7 **7** 7 **7** sts at beg of next 2 rows (71 **73** 77 **83** 91 **97** 105 **111** 119 **126** sts)**
Work 5 **6** 8 **8** 10 **12** 13 **14** 15 **16** rows dec 1 st at each end of every row (61 **61** 61 **67** 71 **73** 79 **83** 89 **94** sts).
Cont without shaping until armhole measures 15 **17** 18 **15** 17 **18** 16 **23** 23 **20** cm (6 **7** 7 **6** 6½ **7** 6½ **9** 9 **8** in), ending p.
Shape shoulders Cast off 5 **5** 6 **7** 7 **8** 8 **9** 9 **10** sts at beg of next 2 rows.
Cast off 6 **6** 7 **8** 8 **9** 9 **10** 10 **10** sts at beg of next 4 rows.
Cast off rem 27 **27** 21 **21** 25 **23** 27 **29** 31 **34** sts for V neck. For round or polo neck break off yarn and slip rem sts on a thread or stitch holder.

Sleeves

Using 2¾mm (no.12) ndls, cast on 47 **49** 53 **55** 57 **59** 61 **63** 65 **67** sts and work 4 **6** 8 **8** 8 **8** 8 **8** 8 **8** cm (1½ **2** 3 **3** 3 **3** 3 **3** 3 **3** in) k1,p1 rib.
Change to 3¼mm (no.10) ndls and cont in st.st inc 1 st at each end of 5th and every fol 8th **9th** 9th **10th** 10th **9th** 9th **10th** 8th **8th** row to 59 **63** 67 **71** 75 **83** 87 **91** 95 **99** sts.
Cont without shaping until work measures 18 **22** 25 **29** 33 **38** 41 **43** 43 **46** cm (7 **8½** 10 **11½** 13 **15** 16 **17** 17 **18** in), ending p.
Shape top Cast off 1 st at beg of next 26 **28** 32 **34** 30 **30** 26 **30** 30 **30** rows.

105

Cast off 2 sts at beg of next 5 **10** 10 **10** 14 **16** 20 **20** 20 **20** rows.
Cast of rem 13 **15** 15 **17** 17 **21** 21 **21** 25 **29** sts.

Front (round or polo neck designs)

Work as given for back to * *
Work 5 **6** 8 **8** 10 **12** 13 **14** 15 **16** rows dec 1 st at each end of every row (61 **61** 61 **67** 71 **73** 79 **83** 89 **94** sts).
Cont without shaping until armhole measures 9 **11** 11 **9** 10 **11** 10 **16** 16 **14** cm (3½ **4½** 4½ **3½** 4 **4½** 4 **6½** 6½ **5½** in), ending p.
Shape neck Next row: s1, k23 **23** 24 **28** 30 **31** 33 **34** 35 **37** sts, turn.
Working on these 24 **24** 25 **29** 31 **32** 34 **35** 36 **38** sts only, proceed as follows:
Next row s1, p to last st, k1.
Work 7 **7** 5 **6** 8 **6** 8 **6** 7 **8** rows dec 1 st at neck edge in every row (17 **17** 20 **23** 23 **26** 26 **29** 29 **30** sts).
Cont without shaping until armhole measures same as back, ending p.
Shape shoulder Next row Cast off 5 **5** 6 **7** 7 **8** 8 **9** 9 **10** sts, k to end.
Next row s1, p to end.
Next row Cast off 6 **6** 7 **8** 8 **9** 9 **10** 10 **10** sts, k to end.
Next row s1, p to end.
Cast of rem 6 **6** 7 **8** 8 **9** 9 **10** 10 **10** sts.
With right side facing, slip first 13 **13** 13 **13** 13 **15** 15 **17** 17 **18** sts of rem 37 **37** 38 **42** 44 **47** 49 **52** 53 **56** sts onto a thread or stitch holder and rejoin yarn to rem 24 **24** 25 **29** 31 **32** 34 **35** 36 **38** sts.
Complete to match left side, reversing all shapings.

Front (V neck design)

Work as for back to * *
Next row k2 tog, k34 **34** 36 **39** 43 **46** 50 **53** 57 **60** sts, k2 tog, turn.
Working on these 36 **36** 38 **41** 45 **48** 52 **55** 59 **62** sts only, proceed as follows:
Next row s1, p to last 2 sts, k2 tog.
Work 4 **4** 6 **6** 8 **10** 11 **12** 13 **14** rows dec 1 st at armhole edge on every row, and at the same time dec 1 st at neck edge on every other row.
Cont dec 1 st at neck edge only in next and every fol 4th row to 17 **17** 20 **23** 23 **26** 26 **29** 29 **30** sts.
Cont without shaping until front measures same as back, ending p.
Next row Cast off 5 **5** 6 **7** 7 **8** 8 **9** 9 **10** sts, k to end.
Next row s1, p to end.

Next row Cast off 6 **6** 7 **8** 8 **9** 9 **10** 10 **10** sts, k to end.
Next row s1, p to end.
Cast off rem 6 **6** 7 **8** 8 **9** 9 **10** 10 **10** sts.
With right side facing, slip first st of rem 35 **37** 39 **42** 46 **49** 53 **56** 60 **63** sts on a thread or safety pin, and mark it with a coloured thread. Rejoin yarn to rem 34 **36** 38 **41** 45 **48** 52 **55** 59 **62** sts and complete to match left side, reversing all shapings.
Joint right shoulder seam.

Neckband (V neck design)

With right side facing, using 2¾mm (no.12) ndls begin at top of left shoulder, pick up and knit 42 **44** 48 **53** 52 **57** 55 **58** 59 **59** sts evenly along left side of neck, k st left at centre of V, pick up and knit 42 **44** 48 **53** 52 **57** 55 **58** 59 **59** sts evenly along right side of neck and pick up and knit 26 **26** 22 **22** 24 **24** 28 **28** 30 **34** sts from back neck. (111 **115** 119 **129** 129 **139** 139 **145** 149 **153** sts).
1st row s1, *p1, k1, rep from * to end.
2nd row Rib to 2 sts from marked st, k2 tog tbl, k1, k2 tog, rib to end.
3rd row Rib to 2 sts from marked st, p2 tog, p1, p2 tog tbl, rib to end.
Rep last 2 rows 3 times.
Cast off in rib.

Neckband (round and polo neck designs)

With right side facing, using 2¾mm (no.12) ndls, begin at top of left shoulder, pick up and knit 31 **32** 35 **36** 34 **40** 38 **37** 37 **36** sts evenly along left side of neck, knit across 13 **13** 13 **13** 13 **15** 15 **17** 17 **18** sts left at front of neck, pick up and knit 32 **33** 36 **37** 35 **41** 39 **38** 38 **37** sts evenly along right side of neck and knit across 26 **27** 21 **21** 25 **23** 27 **29** 31 **34** sts left at back of neck (102 **105** 105 **107** 107 **119** 119 **121** 123 **125** sts).
Round neck
Work 3 **3** 3 **3** 3 **3** 4 **4** 4 **4** cm (1 **1** 1 **1** 1 **1** 1½ **1½** 1½ **1½** in) k1, p1 rib.
Cast off loosely in rib.
Polo neck
Work 10 **10** 10 **13** 13 **13** 15 **15** 15 **15** cm (4 **4** 4 **5** 5 **5** 6 **6** 6 **6** in) k1, p1 rib.
Cast off loosely in rib.

To make up

Join right shoulder and neckband seam. Set in sleeves. Join underarm and sleeve seams.

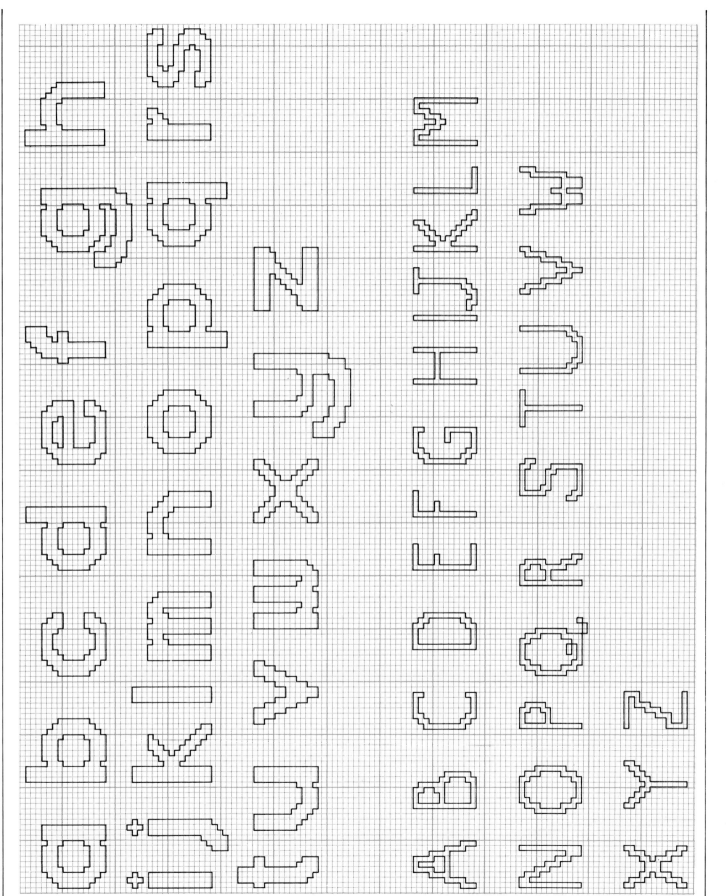

ABBREVIATIONS AND GLOSSARY
of English and American terms

beg	beginning
cast off	bind off
cm	centimetre(s)
double/double (chunky)	heavy weight
double knitting	sport weight
fol	following
g	gramme (1 ounce = 28 grammes)
graph paper	squared paper
in	inch(es)
k	knit
mm	millimetres
mohair	hairy
MY	main yarn
ndl	needle
p	purl
rem	remaining
s	slip
st(s)	stitch(es)
st.st.	stocking stitch/stockinette stitch
tbl	through back loop
tension	gauge
tog	together
4-ply	light weight

NEEDLE SIZES

Metric (in mm)	Britain	USA
9	000	15
8½	00	13
8	0	—
7½	1	11
7	2	10½
6½	3	10
6	4	9
5½	5	8
5	6	7
4½	7	6
4	8	5
3½ and 3¾	9	4
3¼	10	3
2¾ and 3	11	2
2½	12	1
2¼	13	0
2	14	00